Karen Stiller's always beautiful, alway[...] us to reexamine the seeming ordinari[...] new eyes cleansed by tears and in search of hope. From reveries to realities, from hospitality to humility, from giving away to growing up—Stiller pays sacred attention to what has lost our attention and, in doing so, shows us that holiness is here, in lament and in joy, in complaint and in praise. Holiness is our reflection of the divine image in each of us as we strive to discover our truest selves: beings who are beloved and therefore able to love deeply from that first love. Sit with Stiller's book and be still: Holy, holy, holy is this Lord Almighty, indeed.

DR. CAROLYN WEBER, professor at New College Franklin and award-winning author of *Holy Is the Day*, *Sex and the City of God*, and *Surprised by Oxford*, now a feature film

Karen Stiller has given us a remarkable gift in the pages of this book. She has dusted off an old, theological word that can be loaded with misconceptions at best and shame at worst and has polished it into a beautiful diamond of an invitation to pursue a ragged and rough and incomplete holiness in the everyday. In doing so, she has become a trusted and wise companion to all of us. What warmth, insight, vulnerability, and understanding you will encounter in *Holiness Here*. This book has changed my understanding and pursuit of holiness.

JEFF CROSBY, author of *The Language of the Soul: Meeting God in the Longings of Our Hearts*

"Holiness is and holiness does." This is the simple yet profound message of this lovely book. With warmth and wit, Stiller assures us that holiness is not just for the starched and neatly pressed saints. Holiness is for the saints who sleep late, stand in the back of the sanctuary, even weep in the valley of the shadow of death. There are few people I'd trust to tell the down-to-earth truth about holiness—and Karen Stiller is one. I recommend this book highly.

JEN POLLOCK MICHEL, author and speaker

Holiness is a word with gravitas, one I associate with imposing cathedrals, confusing rituals, and formally dressed clergy with unapproachable demeanors. Yet God calls *us* to be holy, you and me. In *Holiness Here* Karen Stiller brings this theological invitation back down to earth, fitting holiness into the spaces between annoying neighbors and messy children, city parks and homemade ginger cookies. If you've felt intimidated by the idea of holiness, I invite you to take a deep breath and pick up this lovely, accessible book.

CATHERINE McNIEL, author of *Fearing Bravely: Risking Love for Our Neighbors, Strangers, and Enemies*

Both challenging and inspiring, this book paints an earthy picture of holiness that you can feel, see, and touch. If spiritual growth sounds, well, too spiritual, Karen shows us how holiness can be found in our reaction to a lost woman on our doorstep; in a big pot of soup that nourishes a weary friend; in comforting a scared child. In this beautiful prose that will make holiness seem a joy rather than a burden, you'll find relief from pretension woven in with the comfort that we can see God, and be his hands and feet, even in the ordinary.

SHEILA WRAY GREGOIRE, author and podcaster at *Bare Marriage*

KAREN STILLER

HOLINESS

HERE

Searching for God in the
Ordinary Events of Everyday Life

A NavPress resource published in alliance
with Tyndale House Publishers

NavPress.com

To our children:

Erik, Holly, and Thomas, who helped us grow

in holiness because of all the love.

CONTENTS

1

SEARCHING FOR
HOLINESS

OUR NEIGHBORHOOD PARK is a city block long and sits across the street from both a coffee shop and the busiest place to buy beer in Centretown, our old and creaky part of the city. I love to walk through it. Dundonald Park on Somerset Street East is hard and soft. Drugs are pushed there, I am sure of it, and so are laughing children on the swing set.

"Is this a good neighborhood?" my mother-in-law asked me.

"Not really," I said.

On her first visit after our move from a suburb to the downtown core, my mother-in-law could clearly see the inner-city mix and match, the falling apart and the building anew, what some people say is good and others think is bad.

Early on a September Sunday afternoon, I came upon a worship service unfolding in one corner of the park. The pastor wore jeans and a purple T-shirt emblazoned with *Blessed*. He preached to a congregation of twenty or so gathered before him, some on lawn chairs as if it were a picnic. Other people lay on the grass or found a spot on a bench within preaching distance, like I did. A loose dog roamed around the perimeter of the group sniffing grass and people, looking menacing in his leather-studded collar. I tucked Dewey, our doodle, under the park bench, just in case.

"We are butterflies," said the preacher. "Transformation is a process."

A shouting match erupted between two women, one who loved the loose dog and another who feared him. One woman shooed him. The other woman took offense. The congregation watched. The preacher's voice grew louder. "Jesus Christ will transform the people in this park and then the neighborhood," he said-yelled. "'Take me as I am.' That's what we are to pray."

Because I was married to a preacher, I was predisposed to cheer preachers on and wish them the absolute best. *This poor guy.*

It got worse. A man joined the ruckus, sitting on the grass with his legs stretched out, right at the preacher's feet. "You're really doing a great job transforming people," he called out. "What a joke."

My pastor husband, Brent, had been heckled before—by a pillar of the community gone rogue on a Sunday morning in a small-town, stained-glass church. The angry parishioner accused Brent of being a fake Anglican because he played his guitar during worship and was preaching about tithing, that ancient practice of Christians giving a percentage of their income to their churches.

"Anglicans don't tithe!" he called out. Sermon heckling always startles, whether it's in a church or in a park.

The park preacher soldiered on. "We can pray, 'Change me!

Renew me!' God's Kingdom is one of light and love, justice and mercy." He took a deep breath. "And now we're going to break into small groups."

The man on the grass carried on. "They sing songs no one knows. I never heard any of these songs. They suck."

The preacher wandered, sharing what I assume were words of encouragement to his flock. The man at the front muttered. Communion broke out, much less formally than we do it at our church with our silver goblets and squares of white linen ironed flat. Here, it was tiny little plastic cups and wafers passed hand to hand. The bread and the cup still stand for the holiest of lives given and received, whether it's a formal moment in a cathedral or a sprawled-out picnic in a park.

The sacrament eventually reached the man on the grass.

I expected him to refuse the bread and body. I thought he would decline the wine and blood, these symbols of old to new, the forgiveness and restoration captured in the most ordinary of objects, a cup and a cracker. I assumed he would want no part of what disappointed him so: the roaming dog and yelling women, the songs that sucked, and the pastor who could not force transformation on anyone this particular Sunday. He was a critic who would never partake, on principle.

But he surprised me. He reached up and accepted the cup and wafer from the pastor's outstretched hands. Then the man wept. He cried like a baby right there on the grass and ate what was offered and drank what was given. The man appeared torn asunder. The pastor knelt down beside him, held him in his arms, and tried to pat him back together.

I nudged Dewey awake and walked home, not wanting to be a voyeur. In my neighborhood park I had stumbled upon the most holy thing I had witnessed in a while.

It is true that we are butterflies—light as feathers, pretty as prayer books. But butterflies, of course, aren't always so gorgeous, and the way to become a butterfly isn't all sweetness and light. You would never guess, until you learn it in second grade, what damp, papery places butterflies come from, what struggle and toil and undignified stages such elegant beauty pushes through. Becoming their new selves takes work and rest, muck and guck, and a safe spot in which to transform until the moment they burst forth with those fabulous wings. They look like an overnight success, but the toil was long and the labor was great.

It is a wonder to learn, as children, what muster and might goes into the art of butterfly making. "Look!" we cry out when we see one. We sense we are watching a flying, flitting miracle when a monarch flutters past. It is all an amazement: the stubby caterpillar, the weird word *pupa*, the chrysalis that is the cage where tissues and limbs and organs stretch and grow, and then, of course, the rebirth into new life, which is where we all want to land.

Transformation is a process. The man on the grass was probably right with all his complaints. The songs here suck. We yell at each other. Everyone else, plus their dogs and especially their cats, can be awful.

But we can be free like a butterfly, the preacher said, a living miracle perched on a leaf, cheering things up.

Some of us can stick a pin in our life map to mark the moment we became a butterfly. The moment we were made new clearly and dramatically, practically overnight. For others of us, our journey to Jesus is a bit blurrier and stretched out. No matter how it happened exactly, we have been changed and are changing still: Jesus made us holy.

We just don't always live or love that way. Our inner transformation from slug to songbird will not always be evident to the people we honk at, and surely not evident to ourselves. We underestimate our own transformation every day by how we act, or choose not to act.

We have been made holy, and we have been tasked to act that way, to live into who we have been told we are.

This is not always easy.

⌒

"This is where your mother and I will be buried," my dad said, his arm waving over a patch of grass near the far edge of the Miners Cemetery in Malagash. It was hot, in that dry, dead way a day can be with insect buzz hanging in the air (and why didn't you bring water along?). The grass crunched under our feet.

I have noticed that the older parents get, the easier they cry, the less they sleep, and the more freely they discuss burial plots. The fathers topple off ladders until you finally convince them to stop climbing them. I moved my elderly dad along in conversation and away from that spot in the small graveyard just down the road from their house.

"This is my friend," he said, pausing at a black granite headstone etched with a single leaping deer.

It was the grave of a German immigrant who had kept mostly to himself after he settled in this tiny corner of rural Nova Scotia. This is a wooded, ocean place where you buy lobsters from the wharf, wine from the vineyard, and milk and flour at an overpriced store in the village. But it's not Martha's Vineyard, or anything like that. Black bears wander. White paint peels. We collect old buoys off the beach that the tides bring in and hang them off our trees.

Here, it is possible to keep to yourself and mind your own beeswax. Dad was an elder in the teeny, tiny church, and this man's name was on Dad's visitation list. Every few months, my father would grab a pile of their church's newsletter, *The Gabriel*, and drive around the peninsula checking in on folks.

"You can come, but don't you come before eleven," the man had warned my dad. But then Dad stood outside the man's house at ten forty-five one day and thought he'd ring the bell anyway. The door opened a small, suspicious crack, and there was the angry eye of the man in his bathrobe. He reminded Dad about visiting hours like an outraged nurse. Dad left and drove around wasting a bit of time in the sunshine. Then he drove back.

"What happened?" I asked, amazed.

"He said, 'Oh, hi, Russ,' and let me in," said Dad. "We sat in his living room and had a great visit. And neither of us ever brought it up again."

Graveyards are full of hard marble edges, but this story softened the whole place for me. To go back the same day you were shut out and not mention the injury or the embarrassment, but to instead have coffee with cream, is holy. It is so very useful. How easy it would be to storm off with your *Gabriel*s and go straight back home to play bocce in the backyard.

Holiness can be daily, ho-hum work. It is often ordinary and right there in front of us. Holiness can have a touch of the monotonous. It might feel boring and invisible, like we are trudging forward and not actually flitting about like a butterfly or being any kind of world changer at all. The reward of holiness might not be obvious to us.

Even still, the opportunities to do the tiny, holy things are right there at our fingertips. We can choose to act like Jesus and not like a big baby, much as we might want to.

⁓

I am a big baby, and our house is an old semi-detached lady with good bones but sagging skin. Her walls are thin. On a recent Friday night, I went to bed early. Our neighbors stayed up late. Just on the other side of our bedroom wall, these lovely people listened to music and walked an elephant around until well past four in the morning.

I had planned an idyllic Saturday of writing, so for most of the night, I lay in bed awake with the knowledge that the entire universe had organized itself against me. I finally hauled myself up at eight to gulp down an Americano and try anyway. But first I stood as close to our shared wall as possible and jumped up and down three times on our creaky hardwood floor, as high and hard as in fourth-grade gym class. Then I slammed the bathroom door like a teenager, in case the jumping hadn't worked.

I did write a few paragraphs, but then surrendered to my fatigue and closed my laptop. Later that day, I called my oldest friend so we could catch up on our news. By then I had started to feel guilty about the jumping. I told her about it.

"So now I'm going to bake them cookies," I explained.

"You tried to wake them, and now you're going to bake them cookies? That is very passive-aggressive of you," she said, like an old friend does.

I thought about it later, as the butter softened on the counter. A soul sensitive to all it's doing wrong is probably a soul doing something right, I told myself. An awareness of our shortcomings can actually help us grow instead of becoming used to reassuring ourselves we are fine just as we are, so very messy.

The ginger crinkles were the repentance for the jumping that had been my revenge. The cookies were a way for me to remind myself that I am to try to love at all times, even when I don't get a good night's sleep. I don't want to be a grouchy neighbor, the mean lady who lives next door and trots off to church on Sunday. I want to be a baker and a maker and a giver.

I sifted and stirred my way through it and talked to my husband. "Do you think this is passive-aggressive?" I asked Brent, while eating spoonfuls of raw dough.

We concluded that if I had baked and delivered the cookies first and then come home to jump up and down and make noise while hurting my feet, that would be passive-aggressive—also weird and not at all holy. Here, the order mattered. Jumping first, followed eventually by shame and regret, then baking. That's holy-*ish*.

This sounds so silly and small, but this is what our days are made of most of the time. The small, the silly, and the splendid. We have all these little opportunities to do something holy and all those big opportunities to do nothing at all. I said sorry, via ginger crinkles left outside their door, for something they didn't even know I had done—as weary as they must have been from staying up all night looking after their house elephant.

⁓

Holiness has a public relations problem, even within the church. Being holy is deeply associated in our culture with being a pain in the butt rather than a balm to the soul. Attach the word *holy* to a person, and even in our very best moments we are more likely to imagine them being insufferable or so different from us.

We have also been taught to accept our whole selves just as we are, which is an important message indeed. We need so much to know that we are loved by God and others just as we are. But we can get stuck there. I can wrap myself up in the feeling that it is okay to be just as I am forever, like a cocoon comforter, swaddled and safe.

But we were never supposed to stay just as we are. We get to change. In that new place, we are loved still, just exactly as we are. The ever-loving God and the ever-changing us.

Theologian J. I. Packer explains holiness as being about the moment and the lifetime. The moment is one of repentance—when "one turns away to God from what is wrong"[1]—and Packer names the lifetime of living into holiness as "consecration," which is a lovely, antique silver tea set of a word that he says means giving oneself to God for what is right.

Consecration is the ship that slides into the ocean after repentance and then sails away on gentle waters and through storms at sea. It is the journey into holiness.

That first moment of forgiveness that follows repentance could be the whole, beautiful gift in itself, and that would be enough for most of us. Some of us set up our tents and settle right there.

Except there is always more. The invitation into holiness is an invitation to a deeper knowledge of God and of ourselves. We were never supposed to stay just as we are. We get to change.

The beauty of our life hidden in Christ begins with our conversion from old to new and from then to now. Now is the holiness part. Because we know ourselves so well, it can be hard to believe that we are holy. We likely feel deeply that we are not holy, even though the Scriptures say we are. We may search for holiness around us in our churches, in our friends, or in ourselves, but sometimes it is hard to see. Our own spiritual growth feels just too slow.

How do we know when we are changing, and if we are living out of our holiness?

I asked Darryl,[2] my friend who has written two books about spiritual growth, how a person knows when they're growing in holiness. His answer was annoying: that you know you are when you don't feel like you are. We talked about the irony that the closer a person gets to God, the more they become aware of their sins. This can make us feel like we are not growing. Darryl said that we can help each other in this journey. That we need each other to help us see the holiness within us and around us. We can search together.

But here's where I want to let you in on a thread that runs through this book: Holiness is not a straight line. It can look more like a scribble on a piece of paper. Our journey to live more fully out of God's holiness and our identity as holy people curves and bends, and we will circle back and go around and take three steps forward and two steps inward and sometimes one big step back. We will jump up and down, and we will make cookies, and we will feel proud of ourselves for doing something that feels good to make up for something that feels bad, and then we might worry about feeling proud. Rather than tracking our spiritual growth as a linear process on a graph with a horizontal and a vertical axis, we learn and lurch as we move closer to Jesus, who is loving us through this messy butterfly journey.

Like the butterfly, our holiness starts in the dark.

J. C. Ryle has been dead for a very long time. In pictures,

the famous author is balding and bearded, with the kind of long, full facial hair my husband, Brent, said he would grow when he retired and when we had grandchildren who would pull it. I said, "Hmmm . . ."

Ryle was an author and minister who came from an accomplished and wealthy family. He became a Christian at Oxford and was later ordained as the first Anglican bishop of Liverpool. When he wrote to his family from school, he described his conversion experience like this: "All these things seemed to flash upon me like a sunbeam, in the winter of 1837."[3] Ryle's life was changed in the flash of a sunbeam, and then slowly afterward for years to come, until he died in 1900. He wrote *Holiness: Its Nature, Hindrances, Difficulties, and Roots* in 1877, forty years after the sunbeam. I finally read it 144 years later.

This thick book is a manual for holiness. It is hopeful and encouraging, and it serves things straight up, as one might expect from a bishop of that time: "The man [or woman] whose soul is growing feels his own sinfulness and unworthiness more every year. He is ready to say with Job, 'I am vile' and with Abraham, I am 'dust and ashes.'"[4] And on Ryle goes, making us squirm.

Because generally, if someone tells us they are vile, we worry and try to cheer them up. "Come on, sweetie, you're not that vile," we might say. Ryle says that holiness, though, begins with these stark and extremely unflattering insights into oneself.

We're not used to that anymore. We want to feel better about ourselves, not worse.

Some Anglican churches are high and feel one pope short of being Catholic, while some are so low, you wouldn't realize you were in a stand-up, sit-down, turn-around-to-pass-the-peace kind of gathering. A lot of Anglican churches are medium rare, combining ancient rites and sacred words with modern music and passionate preaching. And when a new priest rides into town, that priest is wise to not change everything, or even anything at all for a while, but instead observe and know and be known before they start rearranging the furniture. Whatever their tradition, a wise pastor will simply join in for a while.

When we came to the church we are in now, we moved from low to medium, and Brent joined in. Which meant we were praying weekly a very weird prayer that made me uncomfortable.

One day I confessed this to Brent.

"Well, it makes everyone uncomfortable," he said, including all the priests like him who kneel when they recite the Prayer of Humble Access in the middle of the weekly Communion service.

The first time he dropped to his knees with the rest of the priests during this prayer, the top of his head remained just visible behind the Communion table upon which stood the highly polished silver goblets full of rich red wine and the small bowls of tiny white wafers. I had never seen my husband, who was raised in a more casual and, may I say, loosey-goosey style of worship, be so full-bodied about the liturgy. It felt holy, and also a little embarrassing for its bodily boldness. His sudden move surprised me. I worried that his bad knee would give out, and I imagined myself jogging down front to haul him back up onto his feet. Such are the weekly worries of people married to pastors. And then we all prayed these words together:

We do not presume to come to this your table, O merciful Lord, trusting in our own righteousness, but in your abundant and great mercies. We are not worthy so much as to gather up the crumbs under your table; but you are the same Lord whose character is always to have mercy. Grant us, therefore, gracious Lord, so to eat the flesh of your dear Son Jesus Christ, and to drink his blood, that our sinful bodies may be made clean by his body, and our souls washed through his most precious blood, and that we may evermore dwell in him, and he in us. Amen.[5]

It's so blunt, and a little bit horrible, while still beautiful, which is a lot of what church can be, whether it's liturgical in this particular way or not. You can see why some churches do away with this painful poetry, and you can also see why some people sink to their knees to pray it.

The gospel is light and we have shadows, and this prayer brings the brightest day and the darkest night together. We are not worthy, but Jesus has us covered. We are made clean—washed like the laundry that hangs on the line and sways and dries in the breeze—because of Jesus. So we confess our brokenness, always, but we can also pause to appreciate how clean, fresh, and new we now get to be. Growing in holiness is the logical next step.

Holiness is a gift we receive, but also one we give back every day. And not just from sitting around feeling holy—although, yes, it would certainly be easier if that were all it entailed.

~

Consider Peter, the disciple who let Jesus down in a huge, shattering way, and was then rebuilt and relaunched. His story reminds us that holiness is being repaired and then putting ourselves out there again with real, annoying people and frustrating circumstances. Our lives are to be holy in a useful way, and useful in a holy way. Holy is. Holy does.

Peter writes that we must actively respond to God's promises. What is an active response? In the version of the Bible I am currently highlighting with different colors, it says that "God has given us everything we need for living a godly life," which means a holy life.

Leaning in is an active response, Peter might have said. Receive and reflect. Eat and grow. He lists some efforts we are to make, which include things like patient endurance, self-control, brotherly kindness, and love.

Heeding Peter's list is part of our response to God's love for us. It's also good for the world. But the people we encounter will never be the only ones who experience our patient endurance and self-control as a gift: We also benefit from our own efforts. Who doesn't want to grow in peace, contentment, and all the other wonderful things? It is a bit like a list of Saturday chores, work done by us that usually benefits us in some way. Who doesn't love a clean bathroom? "Do not repay evil with evil or insult with insult," writes Peter in his longest letter. "On the contrary, repay evil with blessing, because to this you were called so that you may inherit a blessing."[6] Holiness leads to blessing, we will almost certainly discover, for others and also for ourselves. But it is almost always hard. I fail at this to-do list all the time.

God loves us anyway. We actively love God back by being light in the world, becoming more generally pleasant, loving our loud neighbors as ourselves, and living holy lives, which means doing everything in Peter's list and then some. Remember, this is the Peter who was once very weak, the Peter who is now a participant in his own long transformation. Like Peter, we will find our courage. We will grow our endurance and our endurance will grow us. The caterpillar will become the butterfly. If Peter can change so much by Jesus doing what Jesus does and Peter doing what Peter was asked, then we can all change.

The story of faith is almost always a story of change.

Sometimes we might need to push ourselves a little to *do* the thing that is holy. But holiness is not all about doing, and it's not at all about perfectionism. (Perfectionism killed the cat.) Holiness is about being *and* doing, taking love in *and* giving love out.

This is quite tough, as anyone who has tried it can attest. "Holiness requires us to show our love for God by the quality of our love for others, whom we must assume that He loves as He loves us,"[7] J. I. Packer wrote.

This helps holiness's PR problem: to think about holiness as being about loving other people very well, and not about telling them all they are wrong or where exactly their shortcomings lie.

In the Gospel of John, when Jesus rises from the dead, no one expected it. This leads to confusion, and much running to and fro. Mary, one of Jesus' closest followers, comes to the tomb early on Sunday morning and finds it open, not closed; empty, not full. She runs to get Peter and John, who race back to the tomb. "They were both running," the Bible says, "but the other disciple outran Peter and reached the tomb first."[8] They investigate and then run back home again. Mary stays, though, crying outside the tomb. She sees angels where the body used to be, and they ask her why she is upset. Then Jesus himself is there in his resurrected body. She doesn't recognize him at first and thinks he is a gardener. He says her name, and she realizes who he is. Nothing would be the same again.

In this story there is proof of the great rising—that rolled rock, those linens unwrapped, unrequired, and now lying in a puddle of cloth. There is the mercy of the angels and then of Jesus himself. The way he speaks her name: *Mary.* Jesus is so tender, and this is a balm for when we feel so tiny and tired.

I like that it is a gardener Mary confuses Jesus with: a caregiver to soil and seed, a grower of carrots and crocuses. In her confusion there is poetry because he *is* a gardener of sorts, standing full and heavy in his warm body before her. But he is also just out of reach. "Don't cling to me,"[9] he says, which must have been so difficult to hear. This is joy tempered. Here are mysteries upon mysteries, some resolved, others unsolved, with more to come.

This story tells us what we believe, but it's also a bit of a picture about *how* we might believe and are likely to behave.

There is the resurrection, yes; and then things will be beautiful and still very hard, at once and in turn. There will be darkness and light. We will sing and shout. We will run toward and run away and run in circles. We will weep and we will be comforted. We will be on a tender and first-name basis. We will reply, "Teacher," like Mary did, when we are steady on our feet. Even the racing between the disciples in this passage, with the careful noting of who arrived first, feels uncomfortably familiar. We keep track of each other and tabs on each other, and sometimes not to be helpful.

The Bible is full of people who were accepted exactly as they were, but then changed because of that love. So are our churches. Just ask some of the little old ladies about all they have seen and endured and embraced in their long, gracious lives. We need other people to help us become holy. It's not just you and God, or me and Jesus.

Mary, whose detailed witness rounds out and fills up what we know about what happened that day, was as full of sunny afternoons and rainy Mondays as the rest of us. I suspect her days were not all like a Sunday school picnic after her discovery at the tomb.

We will exclaim with belief and relief, like Mary did,[10] that we have seen the Lord. This might be convincing to some guy on a bus, but maybe not to our very own sisters or cousins. We ourselves will believe but still need to be convinced. We will be buoyed by each other's witness and remind each other through stories and songs; later that afternoon, we will be alone in our own homes, sipping tea and feeling confused again.

We hold within us overflowing cups and dry deserts both. God is always saving us and calling us to holiness. We are always searching.

2

FRUIT

CAROLYN, our church's Sunday school director, stood at the front of the sanctuary for the kids' focus on a Sunday in early July. This is the part of the service where the kids congregate up front for a little story that is often a preview of what's to come in their Sunday school lesson. It's also an opportunity for them to say cute and funny things that give the grown-ups a chance to exchange warm glances and have a chuckle before things get a little more serious with the sermon coming their way. Carolyn held up a sandwich bag filled with gummy worms curled around one another and then a baggie with a handful of chocolate chips. Next was an orange, and finally a peach.

I sat nearby, ready to join the class as a helper once Carolyn had finished and the children began clomping in their special kind of small stampede down the stairs for Sunday school. From my seat at the side of the sanctuary, I could see that a tiny bite had been taken out of the peach. Just one presumably disappointing bite, and then the biter must have set that peach down and wandered away.

Peaches all look the same from the outside, soft orange dappled with warm yellow, fuzzy and beckoning—biting into the hard crunch of an unripe peach is one of life's little disappointments. Those kinds of peaches need more time out on the counter, softening in that patch of sunlight you enjoy when you wash the dishes.

Carolyn played a dangerous game that morning. First, she showed the fruit as examples of what can grow from a seed, but then she planted the idea in the children's minds about how awesome it would be to plant a gummy worm in your yard and harvest a whole tree of deliciousness, or, with one finger, to push a chocolate chip deep into rich soil and grow a bush that drooped low with chocolate bars. The children, starry-eyed and giggling, were thus led shamelessly into a chat about the fruit of the Holy Spirit.

"Of course, we can't grow fruit like that," Carolyn said to the (deeply disappointed) kids. "But God will give you the fruit of the Spirit!" she assured them, and then invited the congregation to call out each type of fruit by name.

Those of us who grew tall in Sunday school classrooms have written the word *love* on the shape of a paper lemon so many times that we can close our eyes and call out the fruit of the Spirit from Galatians 5:22-23 like a wish list for the soul. Love. Joy. Peace. Patience. Kindness. Goodness. Faithfulness. Gentleness. Self-control.

"The mere recital of these Christian graces should be enough to make the mouth water and the heart beat faster," wrote John Stott.[1]

It is a ripe and perfect peach that is more likely to make my mouth water. But when I read that list of the gifts of the Holy Spirit, a yearning to be that way arises within me, which I believe comes from God and is inside each of us. We want to be loving, joyful, peaceful, patient, kind, good, faithful, gentle, and self-controlled. We want to grow. Who wouldn't want to be like that?

This fruit, made possible by the Holy Spirit settling inside us for the long haul, gives us a picture of what a holy life can look like, no matter who we are or where; no matter what we come from or where we are going. We can be loving anywhere, anytime. We can always be faithful, and we can always choose to not shy away from goodness. This is who and what we can be, in the inside and on the outside. This fruit is how we can hope to feel and how we can plan to behave.

God is all these things—we see the fruit lived out perfectly in the life of Jesus—and we can experience this fruit in our own lives as well. We can actively renovate with the One who renovates. We can reimagine our lives with the One who knows all the love we could give, all the patience we could show, all the goodness we could grow, and we can be holy in these clearly defined ways. We can believe these things, then behave in those ways. And we can also act and then believe, in case our believing is sometimes weak. It's a matter of how we choose to live.

What Paul wrote to the Galatians so long ago, and what we called out from the four corners of our old church building on that morning, is possible for each one of us. It's an actual list of holy traits, right there at our fingertips. Those of us who love lists and clear assembly instructions can breathe a sigh of relief. This is fruit that we can both receive and intentionally grow, even if the harvest feels long and slow.

There was a time, when I first walked deeply and finally and metaphorically into the ocean of faith, that I believed (at least) two incorrect things: The first was that we each received one fruit of the Spirit in particular—more oranges than apples, say—and the second was that the fruit we did receive was sun warmed and fully ripe, bursting on the vine and ready to share with the world.

Instead, the whole list is for each one of us, and the fruit may not yet be ripe. I suppose that some of us will be cured of our selfishness the moment we first believe—I've heard of that kind of beautiful conversion—but most of us will spend our walk of holiness squirming to get out of the grip of the fruit's opposites: hate, despair, impatience, meanness, evil, unfaithfulness, harshness, and a self without control. It is in this almost daily battle between the fruit and its rotten opposites where we grow stronger. In our resistance to the wrong and our movement toward the right, we can go further down the path of holiness. Resistance is the path we walk. The struggle does make us stronger. We don't pick up this holy fruit at the grocery store; we participate and toil in its growth. We water and tend, prune and mind, nurture and coax, heeding the clear instructions of Jesus, the gentle (but still fairly straightforward in his directions) gardener of our souls.

My sister, Miriam, has special trees growing in her yard in Nova Scotia, trees she cherishes. "Do you know what kind of trees these are?" she asked me, the least gardener of all gardeners.

"Absolutely no idea," I answered.

"It's a fruit cocktail tree," she explained. "It's one tree that can grow different kinds of fruit."

The branch she then reached out to lovingly caress will, in the right conditions, grow peaches, nectarines, and apricots. Another will produce apples and pears. One single tree can bring forth different fruits because of the miracle of grafting.

Miriam nurtures her trees, like she does all her plants. She wrapped chicken wire around the trunks that look scrawny and vulnerable now but can someday be strong and thick and tall. She protects them from deer and geese, whom she curses as if she's an Old Testament prophet. They wander through her large lawns, grazing on this, that, and the other thing, not realizing who they are dealing with.

"Are you sure you want more than one tree?" the incredulous salesclerk (who maybe should be fired) kept asking her when she bought them. "They're pretty expensive."

I do, my sister insisted. I want them all. She wanted all the fruit she could get and all the fruit she could grow. I admire her thirst and her quest. I want to want like she does.

⁓

Earlier that same morning at church, in a pew near the back, I had witnessed the budding of love in Emilia, five years old, extended to Marilyn, much older. "I love her dress," Emilia said, struck by Marilyn's particularly cheerful floral print. Emilia sat down beside her. She colored and shared pictures with Marilyn, who commented kindly on the artwork. Emilia scooted closer to Marilyn, who beamed. Emilia's mother and I beamed at their beaming and witnessed this nascent relationship between junior and senior make its way into the world on a Sunday morning.

Emilia's very good morning at church continued in Sunday school. Tricky Carolyn set aside her bags of candy from the children's story and sat on her knees in front of the kids, who were scattered around on small red and blue rubber mats. She taught about heaven using a piece of white felt smoothed out on the short table in front of her.

"In heaven, people worship and pray all the time," Carolyn

said. You could almost see the ripple of ho-hum spread through the children.

And then she asked: "Who knows someone who is in heaven?"

Emilia gasped. "I do! I do!" she shouted, waving her arm around. As I observed all the waving and squirming, it seemed that most of the kids, young though they were, knew someone who resided in heaven. Like Emilia, they were enthused. An unexpected celebratory spirit had entered the room as the children remembered people they knew who had died. Strange things can happen in Sunday school.

Carolyn had prepared a river cut out of blue felt to represent the water of life, and she invited a volunteer to lay it down onto the white-felt heaven. She also had a green tree of life, roots and all, which her son Joshua then placed very near the river, which made good sense to me. Carolyn distributed little felt people into every eager hand, which she asked the kids to place in heaven to represent the people they knew, but also, someday, themselves.

The most wonderful thing then occurred. The children positioned their little felt people on the dark green of the very top of the tree of life or laid them down on the river. In felt heaven, there is tree-of-life climbing and river-of-life swimming. Two-year-old Lucy crumpled her person into a ball and dropped her into heaven from a foot or two above. She landed on the riverbank, unfurled, and relaxed.

What place is there that could be holier than heaven? The saints of God are their saintliest in heaven. There and then, they are their best possible selves, which is impossible in the right here and the right now. We know so little for certain about holy heaven, and that will be true until each of us someday arrives. But the people we know who are in heaven sooner than us—our heartbreaking list—have surely now been seen face-to-face and are known heart-to-heart. They have seen clearly through the great mirror. There, finally, they know fully and are fully known.[2]

The children believe all this is so, that God's tender love for us and the holiness which is that love's result and good work will one day mean climbing the tree of life and cannonballing into the river that flows from God's throne. We should say thank you every now and then to the children in Sunday school, for all their certainty and joy.

~

"I pronounce you writer." Even as I said those words upstairs in that same church one morning after service, I was surprised at my own daring. It's not like I'm a writing priest, qualified to make such pronouncements. But as I stood and talked with a young woman who was a writer of skill and beauty yet hesitated to call herself that, I knew she needed someone else to say it to her. She needed to be reminded of who and what she was. We had talked about this before, she and I, about whether—and when—she could legitimately call herself a writer. I thought she could. Writers write. Hannah writes. She overflows with poetry. Her Instagram posts are finely crafted miniature stories of life and love. She is a writer.

But still she hesitated to call herself one. In my own writing life, I had to be paid for my writing for a year or so before I would shyly say, when asked, "I'm a writer." Even then, I would add caveats like "Well, I'm trying to be a writer," and of course, "I'm not paid very much." Or this: "I'm mostly a mother, but I have this little column in the paper. It's just me trying." I would downgrade my writing life so I could lessen any expectations and relieve any pressure to meet other people's ideas of what a writer looks like, sounds like, lives like, and writes like. Plus, I didn't want to sound like a show-off, in case the person thought that I thought I was something special.

We are so shy about what we are and all we can be. Good things feel too bold to say out loud. And if we did, people would then naturally expect something from us. Saying it out loud raises the stakes.

Hannah needed someone to verify for her that she was a writer and to name her identity out loud, telling her who and what she is.

We all need that sometimes, especially with holiness. We need to be told who we are out loud, right into our ears. And if this can happen in a church, all the better. This reminder of who we are helps us know ourselves better and live with a little more freedom and maybe even some panache. You are a writer, now go write. You are an artist, go paint. You are the beloved, go love. You are holy, go try to be even more fully that way. You might even enjoy yourself. The naming is a gift and a push. It says what is true now and points the way forward to what can more fully be.

"You are royal priests, a holy nation, God's very own possession," writes Peter in the first of his letters, to people no better than us, no less ordinary and no more extraordinary, who needed to be reminded. "As a result, you can show others the goodness of God, for he called you out of the darkness into his wonderful light."[3]

God is holy. I am holy. You are holy. It feels scandalous to write that, let alone believe it. Accepting ourselves as holy feels like the most bold and audacious thing we could do. But it can change a life and how it is lived.

Every All Saints' Day, Brent stood in front of the congregation and said: "You are a saint. I am a saint. We are all saints." This was always followed by a ripple of awkward laughter. The "She's a saint, he's a saint, you're a saint" bit was never not shocking.

We are accustomed to thinking of saints as extremists of the faith, women and men who give up everything. Saints live brave lives and die horrible deaths. They are the martyrs who are also amazingly super nice and generous people, a little show-offy with how good they are, although they would never mean to show off— because they are saints! We think saints excel at the life of faith. They will give you the shirt off their back before you ask for it. You want them on a sinking ship with you because they will let you into the lifeboat first. They seem a tiny bit boring, but you don't want to be the one to say that out loud. They provide a hero's story that we can keep at arm's length while we live our more ordinary and realistic Christian lives.

It's simpler and more comforting to think of saints as heroes and healers, and not as Haley, sitting there right beside us hogging the pew. It's easier to think of a cathedral as holy than a tiny hut. We want what is holy to be staggering In proportion and awe-inspiring in height and space—to be other than we are ourselves—because that's easier, and we know our insides so well. We believe that we are not holy, even though Scripture has repeatedly told us we are holy. We have stubborn ears that do not like to hear. We know our struggles, and we see down into the deep well of our deficits. We live with ourselves, after all, first and most and last. It's difficult for us to believe that we are holy, because we are so ordinary. We need to be told we are holy so we can start to believe it. Our ordinariness does not mean we are not holy; it means we are eligible.

Almost everything that becomes holy began as something ordinary. It began as something else and underwent a transformation. Until it is blessed, holy water is only water trickling from the tap into the sink, which needs a good scrub. Bread rises out of yeast, sugar, and flour, and it becomes holy when placed upon an altar. The holy table was measured and pieced together from plain maple and steel nails to be built into an altar at the front of the church, which itself was made from brick and stone and glass and steel. On our kitchen tables, bread is just an important part of a tomato sandwich. But that same bread, the most basic and ordinary of food, is holy when it is picked up and prayed over and torn apart in front of everyone by an ordinary person who was born in Nebraska and drove to church just an hour earlier and said: "This is the body of Christ, broken for you."

If we think we are too ordinary to be holy, then this is the best of news. We are ideally positioned for holiness when we think we are not. We are raw ingredients ready to be baked and shaped and sometimes pounded into something new. We are water and bread and wood. It only takes God to make us holy. The grace upon grace upon grace of the life available to us is that God does the work while we ask him to help us believe that this is even possible, that even we are on the threshold of something new and miraculous. Imagine God's voice at your ear whispering: "You are holy." Then try to say it out loud into an empty room—and it really is best for the room to be empty. Say: "I am holy." Remind someone else who is trying to love and follow Jesus like you are: "You are holy." It will probably always sound and feel weird, and that is fine. It is a holy weirdness. We are weird and holy.

Ordinary things become holy, and ordinary people like us become holy. An Old Testament tent was just goatskins until God dwelled in it, and then it became a holy place. What could be more ordinary than a smelly tent that is too warm when the sun shines down on it in the fullness of the day? With God present, it is holy. In a little corner of Zechariah 14, after you read past the unfortunate section about walking corpses with rotting eyes, there is a more hopeful part of the prophet's vision. He writes that someday even the harness bells of the horses will be inscribed, "Holy to the

Lord," and even the pots used for cooking will be holy.[4] If we can hear it in the bells and see it in the pots, maybe we can also see it in ourselves.

⁓

One night we had our friends Rob and Margo over for dinner, and Rob shared that in Margo's workplace, she is known as the person who always listens. He said that Margo's colleagues at the radio station where she is a producer of a daily call-in show know they can count on her to be there for them, even when it's a busy day. They know she is the one person who can usually be counted upon to hear them out, even if they don't necessarily know that her ability to listen to them comes from her willingness to listen to God. At our table that night, we had just been discussing the long, slow growth we have experienced in our Christian lives. Slow growth is still growth, and the four of us at the table had all been at it for a while by then. We had also been talking about the word *holiness* and how no one wants to use that word anymore, even in Christian circles. We said that holiness just didn't feel like a "thing" anymore.

I could see how uncomfortable Rob's praise made Margo, who clearly didn't think of herself as holy. She squirmed in her chair.

"But isn't that you being *kind of* holy?" I prodded her. "By intentionally taking time to listen to people who need you, and doing it so much and so often that you're actually *known* for your listening? I think that's you being holy."

She swatted the word *holy* away as if it were a fly. "Oh, I don't think that is being holy," she said. "I'm not very holy."

I understood. I would have brushed away the fly too. *Me? Being holy? Nah!*

When we think of holiness, we may not think of joy, peace, faithfulness, love, or patience, and probably not gentleness. Self-control might come to mind a little more quickly when we imagine a holy life, because we often think of holy people as party poopers, not partygoers or party throwers.

The beautiful fruit of the Spirit feels unattainable and even unappealing because it can be unattractive when lived out loudly or brashly. That is a shame, because the fruit of God's Spirit in our lives is beautiful love given to us and bountiful love for us to share. His Spirit can bring joy and peace, which are more solid and permanent and dependable than happiness, with its fleeting, flirty, fickle nature.

God is patient, and his Spirit can give us the ability to accept his patience with us and then be patient with ourselves and, most importantly, with others. God is kind, and his kindness can lead us to repentance, as the Bible says, but it also leads us to be kind in our own lives, to be known at work as the listener, or the person who will lend out all our colored highlighters, or the one who will go the extra mile over that tall hill.

God is good, and his goodness is a gift to us that we can participate in and tap into so that we can be good to others. In a world that is so bad so often, we are invited to reflect God's goodness. This freedom to be good is an amazing treat, better than growing a candy tree in our backyard for the long-suffering Sunday school kids. God is faithful to us, and it is astonishing: the depth of this love that invites faithfulness from us like a natural, ancient reaction. God is faithful. We get to be faithful back.

Our faithfulness to God naturally leads to faithfulness to others, if we let it, because faithfulness means following his commands, which are always relational and involve loving our neighbor. We can be faithful Labrador retrievers, even for just a little while, in the life of someone who needs a friend to bring them their slippers.

Gentleness is a fruit of the Spirit that we can accept and sink down onto so relieved, like a king-sized bed with freshly laundered sheets. And your mother ironed those sheets, as mothers did back then, to make them even better. What would it mean to be holy by being gentle? Or to be gentle because we are holy? These are good questions for us to consider.

Then there is self-control. We can say no to the things that hurt us, even things we might have enjoyed before we knew God and how much better he is for us than that drink, that drug, that person, or that purchase, because the power of the Holy Spirit is now within us, giving us strength and reminding us we are not alone.

Self-control is not just about what we do not do. Self-control is about what we freely and willingly do as we turn toward that other fruit and say, "Yes, please." Self-control can look like saying yes to participating in holiness and seeking where it will take us, like the greatest adventure of soul and soil. What would it feel like to think about self-control as something that can help us not hurt others and not hurt ourselves?

⁓

"You are living stones that God is building into a spiritual temple. What's more, you are his holy priests," writes pushy Peter.[5] If we tried to believe that more, we would act better.

The other day I made a rushed trip to the grocery store. I piled my cart with all the things we needed, made my way through the checkout line, and emptied the shopping cart into our car. Then I parked the cart in the little hut in the parking lot where empty carts belong. As I made my way back to my car, I saw an empty cart abandoned in the middle of a parking spot reserved for drivers with disabilities. *Sheesh!* I thought. I imagined the frustration of a driver who already has physical challenges having to clear their reserved spot of an empty cart before being able to park.

Because I had been thinking a lot about a prayer I had heard in church—one asking God to give us grace to live a holy life—and wondering what that meant for me, I stopped myself from rushing past like I wanted to. I realized I had an opportunity to do something good, which was to participate in a small way in the holiness that has been bestowed upon us. I walked over to the parking spot, grabbed the misplaced cart, and put it back where it belonged. It was a tiny and ordinary thing. And immediately, I imagined someone watching me and admiring my charitable nature. I imagined them thinking I was a very good person. I had to stop myself from glancing around to see who had witnessed my good act. I warmed at the thought of being a good example in the grocery store parking lot.

Is this how a saint acts and thinks? I guess it is sometimes, because I am a saint (isn't that shocking to say?), and that is what happened. But this is how we grow. Doing the right thing on the outside and paying attention to the mountains and the valleys on the inside is being on the path of holiness. We can act holy because we are holy, and then we can ask God to forgive us and help us be better when we don't feel that way on the inside. This is not being a hypocrite. This is trying. It is the effort of holiness that we are called into. The outward act will almost always lead to an inward act of recognition of sin and then repentance. The outward saint and the inward jerk coexist. Then we get to say: "I'm sorry, God, for being such a jerk."

After I helped out at Sunday school that day and saw the children learn about the fruit of the Spirit and then later put their felt people into the most fun parts of heaven, I made myself a list, which I put in my wallet. Love. Joy. Peace. Patience. Kindness. Goodness. Faithfulness. Gentleness. Self-control. They are mine, but not yet fully. They are gifts offered and within our reach. They take practice. Practice always means not being perfect. Practice is an active, deliberate action to improve, which is part of the answer to how we live a holy life.

3

BODY

MAUNDY THURSDAY is one of the least attended services of the whole year, at least in most churches we helped lead. The low numbers were rivaled only by the Sunday after Christmas, which seems to be only for the lonely, plus the people who need to get away from their families for a while. Brent's theory about Maundy Thursday was that this service, which commemorates the Last Supper and the washing of the disciples' feet, is a little dark for some people.

"It's a downer," he said. "That's why people don't come." And the next day is always Good Friday, so spiritually speaking, things only get worse before they get better.

After the Maundy Thursday night sermon, short and heavy, one of the priests reads this admonition from the Book of

Common Prayer: "Fellow servants of our Lord Jesus Christ: On the night before his death, Jesus set an example for his disciples by washing their feet, an act of humble service. He taught that strength and growth in the life of the kingdom of God come not by worldly power and authority, but by such lowly service."[1] And then the handful of people were invited to make their way down front, strip off their socks and shoes, and have their feet washed.

Last Maundy Thursday, I was a last-minute volunteer at the service. I stepped in as one of the helpers who fill the basins with clean water for each new set of feet and make certain there are enough small white towels to dry those feet. *Who would be first? Who would be brave?*

"Sit down and let me wash your feet," Brent whispered. I would be first. I would be brave.

I sat down in one of the chairs facing the congregation, and my husband knelt down in front of me, something he hadn't even done when he proposed on a windy Nova Scotia beach so many years ago. I pulled off my shoes and my socks, thankful they matched, and I worried about the state of my toenails. Brent poured water over my feet from a pitcher I had filled from the sink at the back of the church, tenderly cupping my size nines in each hand. I saw he was good at this. He dried my feet and toes with great care. He took his time, probably being a little theatrical as befitted the occasion, also wasting time waiting for others to finally stir off their pews and come down front.

I found it all slightly embarrassing at first, to do this naked-foot thing in front of everyone. I looked only at the top of his head, bent before me, and not out at the congregation I now perceived as our audience. I admired again his thick, silver hair turned grey early, my own silver fox. It was hard to resist reaching out to touch his hair. We were playing roles, showing that it was safe for others to participate in this ritual, but there was also the presence of love aging well as my life companion set my feet gently back down on the floor, almost as if they were dainty.

I wonder: Did the disciples feel this special when Jesus washed their feet? Did anyone blush? I felt loved and cherished, even though I knew Brent was about to do the same thing with feet he didn't know nearly as well as mine.

By then, there was a small line of people. I filled pitcher after pitcher of water and watched person after person sit down in a straight-backed wooden chair and have Brent or Pastor Michelle kneel at their feet and wash them, like Jesus did for his undependable, tired disciples. That night in history, the disciples were about to fail in the most ordinary ways by falling asleep in the garden and not keeping watch like Jesus asked them. A night that was long and dark and like no other.

I looked it up: the ankle and foot are made up of twenty-six bones, thirty-three joints, and more than one hundred muscles, tendons, and ligaments stretching from part to part. It feels good to have them washed and cared for by someone else, maybe especially by a priest. It is humbling to be loved like that, to have our bodies cared for by someone who is saying to us, through the softness and warmth of a white cloth dipped in water, that we are important, that every little bit of us matters, and that we can serve one another in so many ways, including this one.

We are extremely physical and, yes, so wonderfully made. We are flesh and bone, heart and soul, mind and matter, hand and foot. Our bodies matter. What would it be like to think of our bodies as holy along with the rest of us, even if we use them sometimes to turn and run away?

It can be so hard to think of our bodies as holy places, as artifacts of God's work. The body is how God showed up. Nothing could make a body more valuable than that. These fleshy, lumpy limbs are the dwelling places of our spiritual lives, the sometimes saggy and imperfect homes of our sanctification. These arms and legs, this beating heart and racing mind, are the tools we use to work out our salvation—they, too, are sanctified. Body needs soul to be alive in the world. Soul needs body. We are feet, ankles, arms, elbows, imagination and mind, guts and sometimes glory, and all these parts are one unique and beautiful being. We are the growing seeds and the planting pots as well, a complete and beautiful whole. We grow like flowers.

Our worship is physical. At church we stand and sit, kneel and rise more or less, depending on our tradition. We shake hands and pass plates. Our eyes meet with understanding and warmth. If we are annoyed, or just don't want to speak to Charles that week, our eyes avoid and turn away. We use our voices to sing and say words that remind our minds and hearts how and what we are, together. Every Sunday in our church we recite the Apostles' Creed. We say it out loud together, which matters. Saying it out loud helps remind us of what we believe, of all we have said to be true, even if we don't necessarily think we are believing it on that particular Sunday. It helps keep us on track, helps us gather all our scattered bits of belief onto the same page, at least once a week. It is the north star of all our believing. Saying the creeds and other pieces of worship with others reminds us we are one little body in a big body that spans time and place and reaches back into history to when these events happened in real time, and it brings them forward to us now, here in Albuquerque or Ottawa. "He was conceived by the Holy Spirit and born of the Virgin Mary. He suffered under Pontius Pilate, was crucified, died, and was buried."

So much of our belief rests in the body and has to do with matters of the body.

The recitation of what we believe—the saying of it with our diaphragm that pushes air into our larynx toward our lips, our tongue, our teeth of this body that is holy; the opening of our mouth to say for ourselves and to let others hear with their ears what we try to believe in our hearts—this all matters. It is another movement of the soul and the body entwined, and even more so because we do it in a physical clump of redeemed bodies, a whole gang of us from pew to pew stretching from front to back of this old building. Even if you belong to a tradition that doesn't stand and sit and say things out loud together, you are there and you are watching and listening with those eyes and ears of yours. You are reaching out your hand to take another's as you say hello or say goodbye. You are part of it all. Our one body is part of all these bodies that are Christ's body, the church.

Our bodies are made holy as we participate in the holiness that God gives us. How we use our bodies in the world matters, and how we allow the world to use our bodies matters. Our bodies are part of how we participate in the holiness that has been bestowed upon us and in the holiness we have been asked to live out in the world where we live and move and have our being.[2]

We do wonders with our bodies. We love and give and serve. We open our arms wide, if our arms work like that. We open the doors to our home and wave to neighbors. We set our table and roast legs of lamb studded with garlic that we chopped up on a wooden board that someone else cut from wood and sanded and shaped. The rosemary we grew in our garden sticks to our fingers, which are coated in the olive oil we just rubbed on the meat. We try not to touch our T-shirt and leave an oily mark. We turn dough into bread with our very own hands, after hoping for the best with the yeast. We wash our hands in the warm waters of our kitchen sink. We build tables and paint hills and look at that sparrow in our mulberry tree. We pour hot tea into a cup for a visiting friend perched on the arm of a chair in our living room. We jump to our feet and dance once in a blue moon under the stars at some young person's wedding. We stand on our toes. We pray on our knees, embodied and beautiful.

Within our bodies we feel mysteriously the Holy Spirit's nudge that shows up in our gut and our mind to say something we might never say to a complete stranger or a dearly loved friend. It might be simply "God loves you" or "Do you know how beautiful you are?" Often it is something like "You are not alone" or "I promise that I will be with you." We sit with a friend when she needs us. We use our bodies to love and care for others, like we have been asked to do.

"Lift up your hearts!" the minister says at our church, right before Communion, a bit like a cheer. We say back: "We lift them up to the Lord." We reset ourselves. We pick up on the hint of joy in the leader's voice. We can lead each other in this way. Lifting up our hearts is an act of the will. We might not feel like doing any lifting at all, but we decide to try. Not much that is holy happens automatically, as we will find out (if we haven't already). Someone smart and theological once told me that to grow in the fruit of the Spirit, we must simply gaze upon God and his Word. That has not worked for me or most of the people I know. We can absorb only so much before we must act. To become loving, we must practice loving. To become patient, we must practice patience. Our stiff muscles need to warm and stretch. We will fail and then decide to try again. In our body homes, we will practice the reality of our holiness, together and toward each other and our grouchy neighbors.

With that invitation to lift up our hearts, we are reminded again that our physical is spiritual, and our spiritual is physical. Our hearts are the centers of our physical, blood-pumping selves tripping over our own two feet, but they are also our spiritual centers that fill with sorrow or joy or both. Some weeks these spiritual hearts of ours lie heavy and damp in our hands, like wounded animals we heave upward with tired arms: "Here." We can barely get the words out. "Take it." Other weeks, the better ones, our hearts might float up toward heaven like a red balloon.

～

We are spiritual and physical, and so is our conversion. For some of us, our new state of holiness means there might be a more dramatic before-and-after to our lives than for others, who might have lived a safer or more protected life pre-conversion. In the beginning of our holiness, the visible changes in our lives often have to do with what we stop doing with and to our bodies. Wanting to stop these physical things, and being able to change how we live, is an act of worship. It reminds us and others that God is real and that the Holy Spirit can help us lead a life different from the one we had before. We can become healthier in every way. Just look at us getting better.

The things we give up mean something. They become part of the story we tell, the story about God's holiness and how we see ourselves now. Their absence has an important presence. We can list the changes. The sacrifices we make or the changes we undergo might serve as a line in the sand that we draw with our own big toe, right there in front of us. *Before, I did this. Now I don't do that. I do this healthy thing instead.* Most of us will fail at this. Paul writes about this in Romans 7:15, about his struggles, and it's like we're

41

having coffee with a friend at Starbucks. "I don't really understand myself, for I want to do what is right, but I don't do it."

This giving up of things in the quest for holiness in the body can feel big or little, depending on where life has taken us so far and how we have lived, and maybe even how we were parented or what we did Saturday nights at the Crazy Horse Tavern.

What we put into our bodies, what we do with our bodies, and with whom and when, can all change when holiness welcomes us into the new life it has for us. As we learn what our bodies are worth, we will probably regret some things we have done, and we might feel unworthy of God's specific and tender forgiveness for us, which is not what he wants at all. Shame is not part of God's plan, and shame is not part of holiness. This is the God who washes our feet, after all.

"And so, dear brothers and sisters, I plead with you to give your bodies to God because of all he has done for you," writes Paul in Romans 12. "Let them be a living and holy sacrifice—the kind he will find acceptable. This is truly the way to worship him. Don't copy the behavior and customs of this world, but let God transform you into a new person by changing the way you think."[3] Our job is to let God transform us, but we do have a role to play. There are choices to be made, decisions to try to stick to. Believing transformation is possible will change the way our body behaves in the world, how we treat our own warm, sacred flesh, and how we treat the bodies of other people who become more valuable than ever in our eyes and precious in our hands. We now have the feet of others to wash.

The belief that our bodies belong to God will also make us reconsider things like whether chasing down the car that cut us off on the highway is a good idea. We will ask ourselves where the hot lava of our anger originates, because we will feel it differently.

Where are our volcanoes? What sets them off? Why? These are all questions of holiness that arise now that we know there is a new, better way for us to live. Holiness is a considered path. Curiosity plays a role. Our bodies are good, and we can use them even better for ourselves and toward others. We can ask ourselves regularly how we are doing with that. How is it all feeling right now?

Holiness means being set apart, and this can be a drag. When we start to change what we do with our one very important body— our temple that is always with us and deeply and truly *us* in this soil and sky—we will almost certainly be set apart. It might not even be you who does the setting apart. You might not want to feel set apart, because that can be lonely. But friends, neighbors, and coworkers who find the new you off-putting might set you aside. You might be a drag. It will be okay.

⌐

I took a plane to Florida to care for my mother-in-law after an unexpected surgery. She needed some good cooking and foot massages with lotion, along with gentle pats on the arm. She needed a daughter in law to walk with her to the curve in the road and say, "Good. Now let's keep going to that next tree." And it is always better to flip through *First for Women* magazine sitting in the shade with someone equally interested in the antioxidant properties of berries and stories of amazing living room transformations.

Almost all the way to Florida, I did not act like the saint I have been assured by Jesus that I am.

It began with a woman in the same customs line to enter the US as me. She wore the highest heels I had ever seen. The shoes were black and silver, perfect for standing against the wall in a disco. She wore a loose button-down dress shirt that was buttoned down a good part of the way, and she wasn't wearing a bra, which I could not help but notice. From the entrance of the cavernous room through which the line snakes along like an anaconda until you end up at a small desk for your interrogation by a customs officer, I judged the woman while I tried not to judge her. I tried to feel compassion for her instead of judgment, and then I worried that my compassion was inherently judgmental. She seemed fine with herself. Why couldn't I be fine with her too?

The line was long. The room was packed. I tried not to look at her with my surprised eyes. I stared at my feet. I glanced at the floor and the ceiling, behind me, and up and down and all around me. I watched my hands instead as they lugged my extremely heavy carry-on bag beside me. But because of how these serpentine lines are configured, every five minutes or so you will be standing right beside the very person at whom you're trying not to stare. This is how customs lines move and also how trying not to judge works.

The woman towered over me in the shoes that would break my feet and my neck. I felt short, sneakered, and disapproving, and also very plain, like a pilgrim. A man traveled with her, so I judged him also for the pressure he must have put on his companion to wear those shoes. I tried to not dwell on that. I prayed: *Jesus, bless that woman and her friend. Amen.* Then *Jesus, help her know she doesn't have to wear shoes like that. Bless that woman, who I'm sure is wonderful. Give her a safe trip. Amen.* I worried about her (a little) and judged her (a lot) when really, I wanted to be someone who beamed out rays of love and good cheer in airports.

Finally, we parted ways forever. She was oblivious to the spiritual drama going on right beside her. I carried my judging onto the plane with me, where it joined me in 8A.

"You have a lot packed into this bag, my friend," said the flight attendant whose help I required to heft my bag up and force it into the overhead compartment.

I sat across from a young couple who drank Molson Canadians and vodka and club sodas from takeoff to Tampa.

"I'm ready for the sun! I'm ready for the sun!" the young woman said, again and again. I was jealous of their fun, and of how light they seemed to be.

I stewed like a judge with a gavel in a courtroom. Is it this hard to be holy? Why is it so easy to not be holy? Is judging someone who appears to not be holy a holy thing to do? I don't think so.

My time with my mother-in-law went by both slowly and quickly. After I had returned home, and because I had rearranged work and made poached eggs and avocado toast for ten days or so, some friends told me I was a saint. That is what we say when we can't instantly picture ourselves doing the exact deeply bodily thing that we likely would do, if duty or love called.

"I am not a saint," we will reply, like it's our line in a play. But we will all use our hands and feet and arms and sheer will to help other people—especially the ones we love, because they are often right there at our fingertips. Our bodies will help other bodies. That is part of being holy in the world, and also just human. And maybe being holy is a slow, deep dive into being more fully human? Maybe as we become more like Jesus, we become more like the selves we were created to be, the selves we are capable of being?

Washing someone else's feet is not a prerequisite to being holy—because the only prerequisite is saying hello and welcome to Jesus—but it is a result and a response. Feet can stink; they can be rough to the touch and just generally weird to behold. That's okay. We are okay. Loving what you are doing every moment is not a part of being holy in the world. Doing it anyway is. And when, both during and after, we pay attention to what we are truly feeling about the service we are offering, all the love and the lotion, we come to know ourselves better. We can take careful note, and usually repent.

⁓

Until Brent had his kidney transplant, I didn't realize just how much we are made up of meat and bone, fear and courage. When you move from health to illness, you think a lot more about your insides. You can live with not-great kidneys for a very long time, but not when they're almost completely withered on the vine.

Your kidneys are under your rib cage, on both sides of your spine. Kidneys are the size of a computer mouse. They are small and essential. They are the body's janitors, sweeping toxins out the door.

When Brent's kidney team told him it was time, he told his uncle, who was a doctor, and his uncle told the extended family. The search for a donor match had begun. "I feel extremely vulnerable," Brent said to me, as an email that shared his need for a kidney went out to cousins and uncles and aunts.

Asking for other people's spare body parts is never not awkward. It is extreme vulnerability forced by need. It really puts people on the spot.

We need something huge. You get to say no. Once we knew the letter had gone out from his uncle, we felt naked and needy, at the mercy of the courage and goodwill of people with whom Brent used to jump wildly on trampolines. People he used to push into the lake.

It is best, with failing organs, to find a donor within your family and, ideally for everyone, one who is still alive and well.

But if you're a match, anyone can donate a kidney to anyone. When we first started talking transplant, I assumed I didn't qualify because I had girl kidneys, not boy kidneys. Looking back, this seems ridiculous.

Did I want to donate a kidney to my husband? That was the wrong question. *Was I willing?* Yes. It sounded hard, and I am weak and woozy at body-ish and bloody things, but sometimes life and love require us to say yes when we are tapped on the shoulder. If someone asks you for your shirt, give them your kidney also.

For richer, for poorer. In sickness and in health. We have done all four, and richer and poorer was easier than sickness and health. We met and married as students (poorer), and we saw that, with all things equal and all systems go, we could go up from there. We grew richer, but not *richer* richer. With richer and poorer, there is the possibility of getting a better job, selling some stuff, buying fewer things, going back to school yet again. Flip a house. Get a promotion. Bide your time. You grab the rope and pull your life forward together, like you would a stubborn mule. We grew less poor.

Matters of the body are another thing entirely. Sickness and health is a new country. It goes deeply to the heart of how we love one another, whether we are married to the sick person or not. People who are unwell in their bodies require tender care, and sometimes this country can be a brutal land. In sickness and in health, we learn that our holy bodies can be secret places where things grow in dark spaces where the light does not reach. By now, we all have that friend from Bible study who ate buckets of kale, ran for miles in the fresh, clean air, leaving us in their wake, and still got that diagnosis. Our bodies can dismay us. Our bodies can betray us.

We were knit together in our mothers' wombs, fearfully, wonderfully.[4] But in this broken world, stitches drop and yarn tangles. Our bodies are as broken as anything else can be. We are all disintegrating.

In the end, it was Brent's cousin who donated a kidney. The cousin who was always first in the kitchen at family gatherings to get the dishwasher going. She who would wash other people's large pots by hand, without being asked.

You can be amazed but still not surprised. That's how it was with this cousin.

"I'm not a saint," she said. (Wrong.) "And I'm not a fool." (Right.)

In the days following the surgery, with one of her kidneys removed and installed in a new spot in the front of Brent's stomach, Brent and his cousin healed slowly, then quickly, taking daily walks around the hospital wing. *You've got to get moving!* the nurses said, checking this and that.

We have so many opportunities to live into and out of our sainthood. So many of them have to do with how we care for other people's lives and bodies. There's just no way around our physical selves. We are embodied, and living out of our faith is physically spiritual and spiritually physical. Our saint cousin had seized the edges of an enormous opportunity to give, and she brought it onto and then out of herself. She wanted to restore my husband's body and health by laying down her kidney for him. It felt holy to me and to him.

The body is holy when it is strong and holy when it is weak. When our bodies are coming together (in our mothers' wombs) and when they are falling apart (hopefully much later), our bodies are part of how we act out holiness in the world. They are us and they contain us. It may be that when our body is strong—and this may be when we are young, but not necessarily—we have the greatest opportunity to act out our holiness by caring for others. We can most easily be the giver. When our body is weak—and this may be when we are old, but not necessarily—we can act out our holiness by receiving from God through his people, and growing in dependence on him and the ones he sends to us as his messengers of care and love. We can most easily receive with grace and gratitude.

The last time they were at our cottage on the lake where my husband had spent his childhood summers, Brent walked his mother to the lake down a path he made himself from flat rocks he had gathered around our property. When he was a child, Brent had taxied his mother around these lakes on a little wooden platform equipped with a small boy-sized motor. She is in her nineties now. He found flat stones, filled a wheelbarrow with them, and built the path with his own strong hands so the short walk to the lake would be safer for his parents. On that day, this woman who bore him in her body looked to me like a little bird in a lilac sweater, perched on his arm. It all seemed holy to me then, the woman who had cared for him being cared for by him so very gently. We love and are loved in our bodies.

There will come a day when, for a time, body and soul will separate. The flower will be pulled from the pot. Our holy temples will fall apart and crumble to the ground. We will die. The people we have fed, bathed, bought mittens for, visited, laughed with, climbed up mountains beside, set up tents with and argued with in the warm morning heat, sat and swam with—they will all die. Some of them will be laid down in front of us, and oh, how we will grieve. Even though we knew it was coming, we will hardly be able to believe what has just happened. There will be such desolation. Our still-alive bodies will throb in emotional pain that becomes deeply physical. There is a grief that brings us to our knees. We will have a new knowledge in the very center of our bodies that not everything can be fully redeemed just yet, and we will have to do the work of trusting that redemption will still come, and that our holiness will then be complete. But we're not there yet.

Toward the end of the Maundy Thursday service, as the congregation sat in silence, Brent and the other priests cleared the holy table of any cups, plates, or books. They folded up the white linen tablecloth and carried it into the small back room where things like that are wrapped in soft tissue paper and stored on a shelf. Candles were blown out. Lights were switched off. Darkness filled the church. The priests removed their white surplices and left them on a pew. When all the fancy glass and silver cups and woven cloths were removed from the front of the church, and the cross was draped with a black cloth, Brent nodded at the pianist, who then crashed the keys and created a clap of noise that sounded like thunder and exactly like betrayal. The priests scattered, lifting up their black cassocks and running away. They left the worshipers sitting in surprise, even though we knew it was coming because we have seen this ending before. In their bodies running we saw the disciples leaving and the full-bodied fleeing from Jesus of which we are all capable, until we turn our bodies back.

4

MONEY

ONCE, WHEN THE CHURCH felt like a giant, gelatinous blob oozing its way over every inch and spare moment of our lives, I complained about how many hours Brent worked, and for what felt like so little earthly reward.

"You know, if I were a doctor, I'd be working this hard too," he answered. He said this because, in those days, we knew and sometimes visited (in what little free time we had) with friends who were doctors, or who were married to doctors, or who were doctors married to each other. They had granite countertops and soft leather couches.

"But if you were a doctor," I said, "you would be super busy but then also get to go on great vacations." And have those countertops. And those copper-bottom pots I've always ogled. And not worry about how much hockey costs. And have a more fabulous life in every possible way.

If I thought I were a rare bird in this regard, I would find it more difficult to confess money as a persistent idol. But what is true for one is true for at least a few, and what is true for a few is true for many more, and someone has to turn the lights on in the room. I have never felt I was alone in the misplaced admiration of money. I'm also not afraid to admit this covetousness, because the benefit of transparency and confession far outweighs the cost.

Admitting things to God and others is a way we live better into and out of our holiness. Confession is biblical. Confession cleanses us, like we are little birds in a bath. Secrets and shame are no friends of holiness.

We would all be better equipped to live out our holy lives in relationship to money if we could turn and say to one another, "This is hard," as the collection plate is passed from hand to hand and makes its way down the aisle toward us. Once, I watched someone make change. They put in a twenty and took out a ten. I was embarrassed for them, but I understood.

At our church, when the collection plates are brought forward with just a touch of ceremony from the back of the church to the front, where the celebrant stands waiting, we quote 1 Chronicles 29:14 (KJV) together: "All things come of thee, and of thine own have we given thee." We say it, like we say a lot of things in church, as a statement of what we believe and also what we are trying to believe. *I believe, help me believe. I give, help me give.* Some Sundays, we do mean it with our whole hearts, which gives us hope in our own progress. Other weeks, we might be worrying about paying tuition or paying for lunch. People have left our church because they found the culture of going out for Sunday lunch in downtown restaurants financially oppressive. They couldn't afford the constant lunches at Deacon Brodies Pub, and this made them feel bad. They changed churches because of it. Money can make us all do weird things. Money can make us strange, the lunchgoers and the lunch avoiders.

The heckling heckler who yelled at Brent way back when as he preached about money was saying out loud what a lot of us think. Some of us don't want to release what we have worked to gain. It is ours, mostly. Most pastors will confirm that their church's budgets are upheld first by a small percentage of their congregation who give a lot, and then by a lot of people who give a little. Churches struggle financially everywhere, and this must partly be because a lot of us are clutching our wallets so tightly and our fear so closely. We are all so afraid of being without or having less than our neighbor, and we also want to go out for a great lunch. Jesus predicted all of this fear and confusion when he warned the early disciples and you and definitely me: "No one can serve two masters; for a slave will either hate the one and love the other, or be devoted to the one and despise the other. You cannot serve God and wealth."[1]

This is so radically countercultural, it should distinguish churchy people as deeply unusual, lavishly generous outliers for all time and in all places. I have heard instead that we are the worst tippers at Swiss Chalet on a Sunday. Waitresses can't stand us.

⌒

I was reading an online article about how money quietly poisons our faith. It said that one of the problems with our preoccupation with money is that money creates a false sense of security. Immediately upon reading that, my thoughts turned to the money we have tucked away in an online account. It is a nest egg I cluck over like a mother hen.

I tried not to wonder and worry about it, but I just couldn't stop myself. I clicked away from the article and signed into our online banking right there and then to ensure things were the same as they were the last time I checked. *Yes, it's all there, exactly like it was three weeks ago.* Our account comforted me. The fact that it existed at all reassured me that perhaps we were doing okay and that possibly we could take a trip somewhere next summer. Then I clicked in a little further and discovered we were not getting a very good interest rate, which gave me a shiver of concern. Regret over wasted time crept over me. I started the process of locking things in for a few months with a guaranteed investment account that promised a more aggressive interest rate—until my screen froze in the church library where I was doing my reading about the dangers of idolizing wealth. I couldn't finish the transaction, so I clicked back to the article to finish reading about the seductive lure of money. Where are my thoughts? Where are my worries? There is my treasure.

"Do not wear yourself out to get rich; do not trust your own cleverness," writes Solomon in Proverbs 23:4-5 (NIV). "Cast but a glance at riches, and they are gone, for they will surely sprout wings and fly off to the sky like an eagle."

Stay, little eagles, I close my eyes and wish. *Stay.*

⌒

It is not the wise investing of money that is the problem, of course; it is the flapping of our wings in panic and the nervous counting of our eggs every chance we get that reveals our loves are not in a holy order. Like all movements into a deeper living out of holiness in our lives, our relationship with money can reveal what might need to change and where we might need to stretch so we can grow in holiness.

What would I give away if I weren't so scared? is a question we might ask ourselves every now and then.

Some practical parts of living an intentionally and beautifully holy life can begin with the slight stirrings of obligation. It's easy to dismiss feelings of obligation as old-fashioned rule keeping that hinders our freedom, but obligation can also be an invitation to do something we don't want to do so we can become the someone that God wants us to be. This uncomfortable stretching of the soul can happen with money. We naturally cling tightly to money and all it represents, and we are unnaturally asked to release it for the good of others and the good of our soul. Obligation can be a friend taking us gently by the shoulders and turning us around to face the better direction.

Giving might not feel natural at first or even ever, although with practice it will become easier. This is true of every outward expression of holiness. Holy living is radically countercultural with its deeply relational nature and its prioritizing of the other over ourselves. Care for the widows, said Jesus. Feed the hungry. Clothe the naked. Protect the poor. So much of what Jesus asks us to do depends on our ability to give away so much of that to which we might naturally cling. This is hard work. It might not begin as joy. God loves a cheerful giver,[2] but he still likes and welcomes the rest of us. I know that because I have experienced God's warmth toward me even when I am a grouchy, reluctant giver. Cheer is not the only posture of giving. God wants us to do the work whether we feel like it or not. Otherwise, I'm not sure a lot of us would ever give away anything we would prefer to keep.

The discomfort is an invitation to push in and see what this is all about. Explore the resistance, our spiritual directors say. *What is behind that? Why is this hard? How might it be good anyway?* Giving is a practice because it takes practice. It needs to be practiced. It is okay that we have to learn to give. It's forgivable that generous giving might not come naturally to some of us. Learning to give money away is one of the wrenching and necessary things in our walk of holiness. God loves both the natural givers and those who are less eager, and he invites us all to be transformed and become better at this. Giving experienced as obligation can someday become giving experienced as joyful invitation, which can free us and make us so happy. Obligation can start us on the road to freedom.

The word *obedience* sounds so countercultural now. Obedience is viewed as harmful and not helpful. But of course, we obey all the time—when we stop at traffic lights, stay on our side of the highway, pay bills that are due, or even follow the quiet-time guidelines at a packed campground. Following our own schedule of going to the gym can be a kind of obedience to a rule that we have created. Exercise requires discipline and determination. Some kinds of obedience lead us to healthier lives and a new and deeper experience of freedom. The signposts that lead us in the direction of a holier life—and so many of them have to do with our relationship with money—can help us live happier, more contented lives. And who doesn't want that?

Whom do I serve? It's a holy question we can ask ourselves over and over. It is a question of the soul, for the soul. *Am I serving God or money? Hello, heart! Where are you?*

⌒

When I first learned we were going on a family Mediterranean cruise, courtesy of Brent's generous parents, I assumed that I wouldn't really fit in. Cruises were for older, richer people, I thought, who wear the pastel prints that appear in early January on the mannequins in the front windows of Brock's family-owned department store, and not for thrift-store aficionados like us.

Then I stepped foot on the *Allure of the Seas*, the largest passenger vessel ever and two noteworthy and glorious inches longer than her shorter sister ship, the *Oasis of the Seas*, according to its glossy promo materials. And I met the butler for our hall.

"You'll find us very low-maintenance," I assured him. I certainly didn't want him to think we were cruise people. I didn't see him much after that because cruise butlers work in secret, clearing the tiny sinks of your toothpaste blobs when you duck out to the buffet and whirling hand towels into adorable little animals for your pillow when you're swimming in one of the pools or maybe skating at the rink.

More quickly than I had thought possible, I fell in love with having a butler, in love with his efficient, valuable work. Who would iron for us when this was all over?

Almost immediately, I had become a cruise person. Our kids were also early adopters. When they realized they could order multiple entrees at dinner, there was no stopping them. The waiter in the tuxedo would bring them anything they wanted. Suggesting moderation seemed senseless on the world's largest cruise ship.

One day as I flipped through a glossy magazine, sunning myself on the very top deck, the captain cruised slowly by on his motorcycle.

Back here on land, I still reminisce fondly about our cruise ship with its "soaring new heights" and "dazzling onboard entertainment, thrilling attractions and wanderlust-fueled itineraries."[3] It was hard not to let it wrap its feather boa around my neck and convince me that this was normal life, that we deserved things like cruises.

What does it mean to want things? Is it always wrong or sometimes right? What does enough look like?

Grappling with the role of money and possessions—and a once-in-a-lifetime cruise—in our lives is holy and necessary work that God asks us to do. We wrestle with ourselves and our tendencies toward hunting and gathering, storing and keeping, displaying and showing off. I have lugged three plastic bins stuffed full of my childhood Precious Moments figurine collection from basement to basement for decades, believing someday their value would skyrocket and I could resell them for far more than my parents paid for them. I've made my peace with knowing that this dream is most likely not coming true, but I still have them down there somewhere. Maybe it was my status as a member of the Collectors' Club that makes me cling. As with everything else in our relationship with holiness, we can be curious and ask questions of the position possessions hold in our lives. Asking tough questions about our relationship with things, even cloyingly innocent statuettes and the money it costs us to buy them, can help us.

"How much will be enough?" Brent sometimes asked me as I worked contract after contract to increase my freelance writing income, which would never get us onto the decks of the *Allure of the Seas* but could pay for hockey and ballet and other extras for our kids and family.

"I'll know it when I get us there," I answered, and that ended up being true. I did know when we had enough. I didn't stop trying then or work any less diligently, but I stopped worrying so much. Worry and money are first cousins, after all, which Jesus knew. "Seek the Kingdom of God above all else, and live righteously, and he will give you everything you need. So don't worry about tomorrow, for tomorrow will bring its own worries. Today's trouble is enough for today,"[4] he says, showing how well he knows our flip-flopping hearts.

Today, all by itself, really does have enough troubles. Tomorrow will absolutely bring new ones. Some of what can go wrong in the world will befall all of us. The rain will fall, drenching and nearly drowning us with its icy waters. Our boots will fill with it. Our ships will sink. Despite our striving and saving and squirreling, our money cannot protect us from the deepest pain of the world, which is the loss of love and those we love and those who love us dying and the deep loneliness of being a bodied soul in a world that is not only hurting, but also quite hurtful sometimes. That's when we can so clearly see the limitations of money contrasted with the limitlessness of God.

There is no doubt that money can provide a kind of cushion of comfort after the pain eases up —a good vacation maybe—but it does not stop the continual cycle of gain and loss of love that is our plight. Our lives will be well. Our lives will be unwell. We are between our joys. We are between our sufferings.

Our relationship with money can reveal the answer to the question of whom we trust the most. That is a holy question we need to keep asking ourselves. If we do the work—and for many of us it will be ongoing, almost daily work—of trying to trust God the most, then we will also learn, painfully and slowly, to trust God with our money.

Maybe Jesus was anticipating a day when the world's largest cruise ships would ease their way into the ports of Israel when he said this to his first and later disciples: "Do not lay up for yourselves treasures on earth, where moth and rust destroy and where thieves break in and steal, but lay up for yourselves treasures in heaven, where neither moth nor rust destroys and where thieves do not break in and steal. For where your treasure is, there your heart will be also."[5]

Where, O God, has my heart wandered off to now? On what deck of the cruise ship will I find it this time? It is a wandering old dog of a heart. I will go and retrieve it and carry it back to its rightful place—in your arms.

However little money we have or however sparse our shelves might be of possessions, what we have can become possibility. Our money and possessions become raw material like clay and paint. Our houses become settings for the holiness of hospitality. Our chairs become places for new and old friends to sit, welcomed into our spaces. Imagine what we could create in the world if we all held what we owned with wide-open hands and tried to give like God gives, lavishly and without regret? God doesn't experience giver's remorse like some of us do. Like I did with our cabin.

Years ago, in a moment that came and went so quickly, we did what would now be impossible: We bought a cabin in the woods. At first, we just shared it with mice and close friends whom we invited to squish in there with us. Then we realized how rare and privileged it was for a pastor and a writer to own such a place, so we began to share it purposely with others, and especially with pastors and writers.

It felt like sharing this good fortune and good space was something Jesus would enjoy hearing about. It wasn't a huge sacrifice. To give felt good. I felt generous at last. I patted myself on the back, which should have triggered a soul alarm. And whenever we traveled to the cabin after someone had used it for free, I would find myself checking for things that were amiss. A broken coffee cup nagged at me. My books out of order on their shelves shocked me. Who dares to disrupt the bookshelves of another reader? And who, in the face of such generosity, would use the olive oil and toilet paper and not replace it? Doing something kind and then reflecting on my natural unkindness helps me grow. Giving away what made me want to grab back was an invitation to acknowledge my inner goblin once again and ask God to continue to cure me.

Situations like these are why I don't worry about holiness leading to any thoughts of perfection. What honest person among us could think they were close to perfection? That's just not a thing when it comes to living out of our holiness. I do not have to worry about being too good for my own good. What keeps me up at night is worrying about me worrying about the rolls of toilet paper and who took my books without asking, and then trying to remember to say thank you to God for his tenderness toward me regardless.

Being aware of and amazed by God's generosity and grace enables us to try to want to be givers like that too. For some of us, this will happen quickly. Others of us, especially those of us who find we particularly enjoy a cruise butler, will have our fingers peeled one by one off our very special things and our bank accounts big and small, and walk a longer, more painful road of giving. We can help each other if we can be honest with each other. But usually and happily, a small, good taste of giving does lead to a desire for more. It's good for givers to talk to each other and spur one another on to good deeds, like the writer of Hebrews writes to us.[6]

It is beautiful that as we learn to give and to hold money and things more lightly and loosely, we will be happier people. It's a quirk of giving that what we give away we receive back in contentment and joy. This is such a surprise, like a party thrown for us when we least expect it, and some days when we least deserve it.

That "it is more blessed to give than to receive" is so beautiful and simple; it is a profound counter to accumulating wealth and status.[7] It is an amazingly subversive emotional and spiritual reality that can help us grow in contentment and satisfaction.

We are changed by giving away money and possessions, and the world is made better, hopefully, for those who receive it. It is a holy win-win, and a heavenly math exercise: Me minus this equals you plus that. There is no downside to working to be more generous as we walk along the holiness path. We give. We grow. The only thing that can make it very difficult is pretending that it is not sometimes very difficult. Let's do it anyway.

5

HOSPITALITY

TWO DAYS AFTER MAUNDY THURSDAY, during the Great Vigil of Easter that happens on the evening of Holy Saturday, a woman entered our church like a boxer enters a ring. She seemed ready for a fight. As sparsely attended as Maundy Thursday is—the service that remembers the night Jesus was betrayed—the vigil is like a few friends coming over for a very late-night game of euchre. Hardly anyone shows. People who join our tradition and are new to liturgical life are usually still so bummed out after Maundy Thursday and Good Friday that they might not believe us that Saturday night is not just another exercise in desolation. By the time the woman arrived, we had already lit our candles from the small fire built in the alley beside the church. We were already listening to a litany (an actual litany) of readings from the Bible.

She stomped loudly through the church, trying out one pew after another. The woman seemed to inhabit an otherness from the rest of us, who appeared more settled and more warmly clothed.

This was the "most holy night, in which our Lord Jesus passed over from death to life," as the prayer book says, and "the Church invites her members, dispersed throughout the world, to gather in vigil and prayer."[1] The service grows out of the bleak and cold soil of Good Friday and ends close to midnight on the day before Easter morning, with a springtime-like lift of the hearts upward. There are even bells rung by people who either brought them from home or selected them from a cardboard box at the back of the church. Holy Saturday is a wilderness of a day. It's a relief when it draws to a close with bells. Besides, few things are more lovely than an Anglican lady vigorously ringing a little silver bell late at night, smiling at the people around her.

Our guest had slid into a pew and sat right beside Julia and Hannah and directly behind my daughter Holly and me. Waves of what felt like aggression rolled out from the woman, along with discomfort from the rest of us, even though we tried not to feel that way. The woman seemed angry. She muttered. She thumped. I worried. The visitor moved into our pew then and lay down on her side, her hands folded under her head. It was time for a hymn. Hannah and Julia both sing beautifully and, standing in the pew behind the woman, sang over her like an unplanned lullaby.

The woman fell asleep almost immediately. She snored loudly and shifted around on the pew, probably trying to get more comfortable on that polished wooden bed. Holly walked through the darkness of the church to the library down the hall, with all its books of wisdom and guides to spiritual living, and found a red-velvet cushion that she brought back and laid beside the woman's arms. A few moments later the woman moved it under her head as a pillow, which was what Holly intended. She slept through the canticles right into the confession, and in her sleep, we hoped she felt safe. In all the places in all the world, she should feel safe sleeping on a church pew late on this unordinary Saturday night. We welcomed her, in our fretting, clumsy way, and she trusted us in her slumber, or so it seemed. This felt like hospitality given and received, flowing in imperfect fits and starts among all who were there in the church on that night, on the eve of Easter.

⌒

Hospitality is holiness lived out in practicality. It is the pillow, the food and drink, and the hot shower of our practical love. The spiritual is practical. The practical is spiritual.

The Holy Trinity is a mystery to me, with its three-in-oneness and its oneness-in-three, and I can just barely grasp the deep relational nature of how the Father, Son, and Holy Spirit touch and spin and dance off each other and with each other. Hospitality— that generous making room for others and giving and receiving to and from each other from our plenty and sometimes from our scarcity but we do it anyway—seems to flow out of that communal and relational and so generous nature of God. Being holy as God is holy, if we can believe it, catapults us into relationship with others and the practice of hospitality. Holiness is relational, and that is why hospitality fits holiness like a soft leather glove.

All of this is made easier alongside the holy practice of gratitude. I have this place, this food, this book; please take it and enjoy it as well. We try to believe that everything we have comes from God, and so it is ours not to own but to share. Here—a red-velvet pillow just for you. Take it with you if you want. So hospitality is almost always best when it is gratitude adjacent. However, the discipline of hospitality can happen also while you are still a grouchy, miserly mess. Disciplines take discipline. Not everything is easy or feels good right away, but that might mean it's even more worth doing, and not less.

~

In Luke 14:12-14, Jesus tells us how to throw a dinner party. Dinner parties are, after all, what most of us think of first when we think about hospitality: "'When you put on a luncheon or a banquet,' he said, 'don't invite your friends, brothers, relatives, and rich neighbors. For they will invite you back, and that will be your only reward. Instead, invite the poor, the crippled, the lame, and the blind. Then at the resurrection of the righteous, God will reward you for inviting those who could not repay you.'" In 14:8-10, he even discusses seating plans: "When you are invited to a wedding feast, don't sit in the seat of honor. . . . Instead, take the lowest place at the foot of the table."

Jesus knows me so well. He predicts my thirst for status. When we practice hospitality as part of our holiness, we will come face-to-face with our desire to invite first our friends, the people we especially like or those whom we want to especially like us, along with the relatives we are most comfortable with, and, of course, our rich neighbors. We might strut around like a peacock in our own dining room and not even realize we are doing it. Again, our intentional moves toward holiness will show us how far we have yet to travel. Our efforts to do good on the outside will show us how far we are from good on the inside, and in that gap, we learn again of our need for the forgiving, restoring love of God in our own lives and hearts, and how much we need him, even when we are serving macaroni to friends.

We learn something about ourselves—and therefore move deeper into our holiness journeys—when we pay attention to whom we want to welcome in and how we want to welcome them to our homes, our tables, and our lives.

As we consider ourselves, we can confess ourselves to God and ask for help.

Why am I making this so fancy? we can ask our inner hostess, in an examination of motivation that is a daily part of pushing into our holiness. *What is my motivation?* Also, *Why am I talking about myself so much? And why can't I stop?*

Our honest answers do not bring the dinner party, the coffee date, or the open house to a screeching halt, but instead provide us another opportunity to be honest with ourselves and with God— who is the ultimate and gracious host of heaven and earth now and the new earth that is to come. *Make me holy in my hospitality,* we might pray. *Kill off my show-offness,* we might ask. *Help me listen more than I speak, as my blunt spouse has said I need to work on.*

Help me not to be so needy, I can pray as I juice blood oranges for udon noodles with fried tofu and orange nam jim from my expensive hardcover *Ottolenghi Flavour* cookbook propped open on the counter.

Perhaps for a little while, as part of our own healing, we will make a simple spaghetti Bolognese, accept the offer of our guest to bring store-bought garlic bread, and let Maureen help with the cleanup, like she always wants to do. We will resist the temptation to offer our guests a tour of our new barbeque and satisfy our thirst for thanks by turning it outward to gratitude to God. What if whenever we yearn for someone to say, "Thank you, you are marvelous for all you have done," we accept that as a prompt to whisper, "Thank You. You are marvelous for all You have done."

Food is just one expression of hospitality. Conversation is

another. When we practice holiness through hospitality, we create a space in which other pursuits of holiness can be practiced, such as listening well and not interrupting, putting others first, and offering encouragement and companionship to the person God has placed and we have invited in front of us. From the way Jesus tells us to invite, and the humility presumed in his recommended seating plan, we can assume that we don't invite people to our table so we can imprison them to hear all and only about us. We don't tie them to their chairs with our story and our glory.

We can practice patience, a fruit of the Spirit we get to work with, toward friends who arrive late (or even worse, early) and those who stay too long. We practice not biting off the heads of those with whom we disagree. If we do bite their heads off at dinner, we can practice the art of unequivocal apology. Apologizing is a holy act. *I'm sorry* are holy, healing words. Through hospitality's gift of space opened up and time slowed down, we can "be happy with those who are happy, and weep with those who weep," which Paul told us to do only two verses after he reminded us to "always be eager to practice hospitality" in Romans 12:13-15.

It might feel better to wait until we want to do things before we do them. But in the pursuit of holiness in daily life, that is just not the way. Holiness grows in the sweat of effort. There is redemption in the resistance. Living a holy life can be like going to a spiritual gym for a Tuesday noon workout. The acting out of our holiness is a decision like love. Sometimes we think that if our motivation is not correct, then we aren't yet ready to do the hard thing, or that we aren't capable. Or we think we just shouldn't put ourselves through things that are uncomfortable or that don't feel true to ourselves. We don't like to stretch or groan in misery even for just a moment, or to vacuum the house. We believe that hospitality is for others who are already good at it, who are saintlier in all the obvious ways, and have tidier, tasteful places. Very few pots of spaghetti sauce would ever be made (or opened and poured into a pot to heat and spit all over the stove) if this were the case.

Moving against the impulse toward our own comfort can be part of how we grow and become our best selves. What if we are shortchanging ourselves when we don't stretch ourselves? It is not inauthentic to our true selves to do hard and holy things. It might even be the path to our truest selves. We discover we are capable of the hard and the holy, and we grow through doing those things. If you happen to be the person who usually does all the busy work of hospitality, you can help your partner grow in holiness by giving them some of the chores also. Come and be holy with me in the kitchen, you might say. If you're part of the team, use the team. You don't have to do all the work, after all.

It is work. It's work to push through and do it anyway. A more magical way to grow would be easier, but it is the grit of the sandpaper moving against the wood that makes it smooth. I know this from watching my father build things.

Egg whites become velvety soft peaks perfect for meringue only when they're vigorously stirred with a wire whisk, a determined hand, and a set mouth. I know this from watching my mother bake things.

Very few of us are as naturally sweet as pie. We know this from watching ourselves. But being sweet as pie is not required to bake one. For that, you need flour, shortening, sugar, and a filling. If we don't love our friend, who seems to need a pie today, we remember that we do love Jesus, and that is where we always and best begin.

I want to close my door instead of opening it. I am so busy. I am so lazy. If I wait until I am healed on the inside, I will never make another lasagna, and I will miss so very much.

~

Hospitality is one of the best parts of the adventure of holiness, so rich with possibility. Hospitality as time and space offered between us creates joy and tender surprises. Who knows what could happen here and now, or in the next few hours? Who can guess the revelations, words of wisdom, and funny stories that will be shared? What wounds might be healed? What fun might be had? Jesus was always eating with groups of people. We can imagine him listening and laughing, asking questions, and exchanging stories. Sitting up and leaning back, leading and then following the conversation. In John 21:9, the disciples "found breakfast waiting for them—fish cooking over a charcoal fire, and some bread." Here the resurrected Jesus reminds me of a mom, clucking just a little bit: "Now come and have some breakfast!" Jesus says (21:12).

Years ago, we held an open house during Advent for people in our church. Every year we would invite members of our church to come to the rectory and gab over a table full of appetizers. Eventually, we realized we were hosting people closest to us who were familiar and comfortable, and not our neighbors whom we did not know and who didn't already attend our church. By inviting church people, we built goodwill and strengthened community within the church, which was all good. But it was also a clear reward for our hospitality. Our open house felt churchy, but not biblical. We decided to do what Jesus suggested and invite people with whom we didn't have an agenda of community building and from whom we didn't expect anything in return. We printed invitations and stuck the papers in doors and mailboxes, not knowing who might show up—if anyone.

Hospitality always carries with it the risk of humiliation, which helps with humility, which is another holy thing.

One of the first things we learned from our neighborhood open houses, which ran for about four years until we moved, was that most people already knew each other. We were the ones who weren't really part of the community on our busy street. We hadn't lived there long enough, or invested the slow time it takes to know neighbors beyond a wave from a window or a nod on the sidewalk.

Mary, who lived on the corner and was newly widowed, arrived alone. Her loss was fresh, and she carried her grief with her like a heavy bag. The couple who always waved vigorously to me from their bay window also attended. Sometimes I walked a different route home with my dog, to avoid their eagerness and what I sensed was a deep loneliness. Two of their children had died years ago, they had told us, one from a hit-and-run, the other from an asthma attack. Their losses reminded me that such losses are possible, and my impulse was to avoid them. That's what non-grieving people often do with grieving people. Blessed are the people who have really sad people over for a cheese ball.

Trying to avoid sad people and heartbreaking topics works against the practice of hospitality. Certainly, it is more work when the guests cry. It is more pleasant to rejoice with the rejoicing than weep with the weeping. That night, we did start to talk about sad things in our living room.

I don't remember exactly how the conversation turned from Christmas plans to grief, but people began to talk about loss and to remember their children out loud. One of our neighbors began to cry. He was a tough guy, and his tears surprised him and the whole room.

"We're all in the same boat," observed Mary, the new widow. Everyone in the room did seem to be carrying a weight. "Can we sing now?" she asked Brent. We had introduced caroling the year before, and it had been a surprise hit.

Brent began to sing "O Come, All Ye Faithful" with his beautiful voice. Our neighbor man cried on. The mother from the bay window walked over to him, wearing the furry slippers she brought with her, in what seemed to be her practical way. She put her arms around him and rocked him back and forth. She murmured to him as a mother does. We sang on, as if we were a slightly off-key soundtrack to a small healing.

That night, we had filled the punch bowl, arranged some chairs, and lit the candles. Then God became the actual host of the evening. God will do that, when invited. When we have the courage to sit in rooms together, even with near strangers who are neighbors, we can see that we do sit in the same boat with all its possibilities and dangers, its blessings and its snares, all of which we can better bear together. This, too, is holy.

As the Gospel of John winds up, and after Jesus has served the disciples bread and fish on the beach, he turns to Peter and asks him three times if Peter loves him. It's hard to imagine the anguish Peter would have experienced over his betrayal of Jesus during the awful days before. Shame can get in the way of the enactment of our holiness. We think we are not good enough or ready enough to do the right and holy thing. Shame can hold us back. Peter would have felt the grief of his betrayal and the loss of Jesus as a physical pain. His unholy shame would have been a hard ball in his stomach. It's hard not to think of him as the first anxious disciple. There, on the shores after breakfast, is the beautiful restoration of Peter. Three times he denied Jesus, and three times he is given the opportunity to reaffirm his love and devotion. This liturgy of forgiveness unfolded in the embrace of hospitality offered by God himself, who did not view the preparation and offering of food as something beneath him, but humbled himself, and cooked breakfast on the beach.

⁓

Hospitality is woven into the fabric of the universe. It's how we relate to one another. When we practice hospitality, we extend welcome to one another in an ancient liturgy of giving and receiving that precedes Creation: "In the beginning the Word already existed. The Word was with God, and the Word was God."[2] Hospitality has always been about relationship. It's never been just about ordering pizza.

We receive holiness from our relational God, through nothing we have done or will ever do to deserve it, because God is the ultimate giver. Made holy through God's hospitality, we can then learn from Jesus how to make our holiness come alive, which will be a trial-and-error kind of experience, full of bumbles and misses and, thankfully, the occasional moment of getting it right.

Holiness is not just about being; it is also about doing. Holiness is and holiness does. We are in relationship with Jesus, and now we get to be in relationship with others all around us. We get to weep with those who weep and rejoice with those who rejoice. The weepers and rejoicers will do the same for us, because rejoicing and weeping will find us all, eventually. The sharing of the experiences that make us human and help us grow in holiness happens very naturally through the holy practice of hospitality.

We don't have to worry about our practice being perfect. Practice is always incomplete and imperfect; an act of becoming and of creativity. Practice is showing up and not giving up. It is movement toward holiness, however clumsy.

The doorbell rang one Wednesday afternoon in February, and I discovered a weary-looking woman on our front porch. There were several large and worn suitcases, and mounds of plastic bags overflowing with sweaters, shoes, and magazines piled around her.

"Hi!" she said. "I'm here to move in."

"Um, I'm not sure," I answered, trying to make sense of the scene in front of me. "I wasn't really expecting you."

She confirmed our house number, which was correct.

"Just my husband and I live here," I said. "I'm sure you're wonderful, but I'm positive this is not where you're supposed to be." The woman dug in the pockets of her winter coat to find a crumpled piece of paper, her destination scrawled on it in pencil. She and I—and the taxi driver who continued to unload more stuff onto our steps—then all agreed she had arrived at the wrong house on the right street, and that her real destination was 282, not 262.

"Well, good luck," I said, and closed the door against the winter chill and the woman who would not be my roommate. I wanted to get back to my laptop on the dining room table, where I was editing an article about something spiritual.

From my quick impression, I believed the frazzled woman on my step might have bigger challenges than arriving at the wrong house, and that the address on the paper was likely one of the rooming houses on our downtown street.

I had closed the door confident I was not called to invite her to move into our spare bedroom. "Surprise!" I imagined saying to Brent when he returned home from his church office later that day. "We have a new complete stranger living with us." The woman probably would not want or need that anyway. She would have found us boring.

But we are supposed to be different. I hurried back to the door, pulled on my boots, and went outside to help the woman carry her belongings back into the open trunk of the taxi. If I couldn't invite her in, I could at least help her out.

"You don't have to do that," she said. And as I hauled the last few plastic bags down the steps anyway, it occurred to me that my small gesture might appear as if I were rushing her along, impatient to have her gone from my step and my day. Also, maybe she didn't want my hands all over her stuff. This might have backfired.

It was all a bit of a bungle, and a misfired attempt at stirring myself out of my comfort zone and trying to do what Jesus might have done. I know that it's extremely easy to do nothing, so I was glad I had done something. I didn't want to shut our doors and focus only on my own family and life, and on my own spiritual growth. Our call to holiness will always lead us out of our padded shells and into a hurting, challenging world.

I vowed to myself that I would watch out for the woman, whose name I didn't think to ask, and be friendly if we passed on our shared street. I haven't seen her again. I will keep my eyes open.

6

HUMILITY

WHEN I WENT BACK TO SCHOOL at midlife, I returned to the campus that housed the tiny chapel in which Brent and I had married. One day, as I sat on the library stairs and ate a money-saving sweet potato I had brought and microwaved for lunch, a classmate wandered by and asked if I would show her the chapel. I had told my writing cohort how pretty it was and what a lovely spot it had been for a wedding thirty years ago.

"Sure!" I answered my new friend. "That would be great. I'd love to show you."

As we walked into the small church together, the thought unfolded within me that I must have done something right to have nurtured this interest within my new friend to tour the chapel. And after only one week in class together! Now here she was beside me, interested in church. And therefore, I concluded, the Christ light must have shone very warmly within me. I was nervous about how I would share my personal faith with her (I was so rusty!), but also pleased to have this opportunity, because I had clearly shown myself to be normal and nice. That had been the low bar I had set as a Christian writer in a secular master of fine arts program. Be normal. Be nice.

We entered the holy space together. Dust hung in the streams of light coming through the windows. Gloomy photos of past rectors were hung too high across one wall. There before us was the aisle up which I had marched to the beat of a small congregation gamely singing, "Praise to the Lord, the Almighty, the King of creation!"

"What's this?" my spiritual protégée asked, as she paused at the baptismal font. I tried to explain baptism and how water marked the new life given to us by Christ. It sounded a little strange even to my Christian ears. She asked a few other questions as we wandered around. She picked up a hymnal and flipped through it. The tour was starting to lag a bit.

It occurred to me then that she might have been trying to think up questions to ask, and suddenly I knew—in the way you really know that now you really know—that we were not in the chapel because of the winsomeness of my faith but because of the kindness of my friend. She saw me with my potato and took pity. She recognized my solitariness and reached out and in.

She was the one being kind to me because she was kind, not because I was a super Christian driving her down the love highway. And so, in this way, and as we often are, I was humbled.

Sometimes we learn humility because we seek it. More often, it finds us sitting around thinking we are a little bit fabulous.

To seek fullness to our holiness is to live with humility. There are pivotal moments in our spiritual journey when we remember we are not as good as we thought we were, and important moments when we learn we can be worse than we feared. (There will also be glimpses of sunlight, don't worry.) But knowing and accepting our raggedy selves and souls doesn't mean we are being down on ourselves, necessarily. It means we have seen ourselves clearly in a mirror, and not dimly, because it is ourselves we are looking at. We are faced fully with ourselves, and the upside is that we can experience even more the tender and fierce love Jesus has for us. His love is even warmer and more welcome when we see our own lack and don't try to cover it up by making excuses or blaming others for our own shortcomings, which sit there like birds on a wire, if we open our eyes to see.

We are necessarily humbled at the beginning of our journey, in the dirt at the foot of the cross. It is God's kindness, yes, but also coming to the end of ourselves that leads us to repentance. We will be humbled again and repeatedly in living rooms, on baseball diamonds, along forest paths, and in quaint chapels. Our humbling can take place anywhere and anytime. It's a bit of a free-for-all.

Our great and tiny and repeated humbling is part of the nonlinear growth path of holiness. As we try to do a holy act—maybe by making some gesture of kindness toward someone or by showing extraordinary patience when we could have instead bitten someone's head off—we might glimpse our own mixed motivation or feel disappointed in how much work it is to do the holy thing after all. We thought we were better at this than we are. We hoped it would feel better. Perhaps we grew impatient with the person we wanted to help, and then were saddened by that feeling inside us.

One of the first times I served at a weekly dinner for people living in economic need, I wanted to be thanked. I didn't go into the hall that night and tie on the apron to be thanked. I thought I stirred the soup and ladled it into bowls to feed the hungry. I cut bread into slices because I thought the reasons for poverty were complex and often systemic, and that those who had more security in that given moment should give to those who didn't. At least, that's what I told myself. But really, I also wanted to feel good and be seen and receive thanks. The holy act of serving food to those who needed it on that night revealed to me my inner state more clearly, and therefore gave me the opportunity to tell God that I was sorry and continue to serve anyway. Serve and grow. Grow and serve. Say sorry.

We do not grow in a straight line. Holiness can't be charted out on graph paper, although that would be easier and so much more predictable. The journey into our holiness so we can live out of our holiness is more loop than line. Holiness is in and out, backward and forward, around and around, then out a bit farther, and in a bit deeper. Three steps forward and two steps back, exactly like our mothers described our progress in other things, with that sigh.

Our outer acts of holiness (which we have been instructed to do) and our inner selves (which we are advised to pay close attention to) will rarely match up, at least at the beginning. The beginning can be long. The deeply inadequate ways in which we practice holiness in our lives and in the world will always, inevitably, involve humility. As we trip over holiness, we tumble into humility. We will do right and holy things on the outside while sometimes thinking and feeling wrong and unholy things on the inside. Does this make us hypocrites? No, this makes us people who are trying to do as we are told and have been asked.

A perfect alignment between outer actions and inner feelings will be rare, for most of us, although we can grow better at that through the looping, curving walk of the practice of holiness. Humility is baked directly into this cake.

When we try to love out of our holiness, and find we cannot easily do it, or that our attempt at selflessness reveals to us our selfishness, we are humbled. Our sin startles us once again. This can be a gift if we allow it to be. We learn again that we can't do holiness alone. We need Jesus to help us, please. The humility that leads us into greater dependence on Jesus as the source of all our holiness helps us grow. We are reminded, again and again, that left to our own strength, we are weak. Left to our own devices, we are deviceless. These moments of clarity into our own spirits can discourage us if we let them, or we can wrench ourselves around and ask God to help us see them as opportunities for repentance and growth. We can try to be thankful for the mirror that has been held up.

Our temptation is to share holiness by talking about it instead of doing it. But we can't spread holiness around like butter. We are not the saviors of the world. Not everyone wants what we have to offer with all our buckets full of it. It is ours to hold lightly, not to share heavily. People don't necessarily want our opinions on how to make their lives better, even if we think we know. Sometimes it might feel as if no one at all is interested in having us as their know-it-all tour guide through tiny chapels. Our job is not to make other people live like us, but to love those we encounter as we encounter them, which is exactly how we ourselves wish to be loved, of course. I can't think of a single person who wants another bossy judge in their lives, but they might welcome a friend.

"You are the salt of the earth," Jesus said to his disciples then and now. "But if the salt loses its saltiness, how can it be made salty again? It is no longer good for anything, except to be thrown out and trampled underfoot." He added, encouragingly, I think, that we are also "the light of the world," shining our light before others so "that they may see [our] good deeds and glorify [our] Father in heaven."[1] Salt and light can so easily be too much or too little. When they're in the right amounts, they are usually just there quietly doing their work of salting and lighting, without being overbearing or blinding. In the right amounts, salt and light make things better for everyone who is at the table or in the room, or just looking for deliciousness and a way forward. Notably, Jesus did not ask us to be like marching bands, crashing in with our noisy gongs and clanging cymbals.

⁓

I sat for a while one morning in the deserted eating area of a Hampton Inn where I was on an extended stay accompanying one of our children for medical treatments. I was reading Frederick Buechner's *The Alphabet of Grace* and carried it with me down to the free breakfast I had grown to enjoy very much. Those piles of round and delicious sausage patties and the endless supply of ice-cold orange juice in my little plastic cup beckoned me each morning. Buechner had died just a few weeks before, so I was filling in my book gaps, as readers do when writers die. I was having occasional conversations with the woman who vacuumed the floor and wiped the tables. We shared an electrical plug in the wall so

I could charge my phone while I gorged on book and meat and juice, and so she could reach the tight corners of the room with her vacuum. Her plug fell out again and again. I plugged it back in. She thanked me. I felt pleased. There was a reading-vacuuming kinship in the room, at least for me, the one sitting and reading.

Buechner was describing a friend who made the sign of the cross before she started her daily writing. This appealed to Buechner, and it did to me as well, just reading about it that morning. I've always wanted to be someone who makes the sign of the cross both before and after they do things. All kinds of people in our church cross themselves during the service. It's that kind of a church. They do it when they say amen. When they pass before the cross up front, they pause, turn, and cross themselves, while I stomp past like a heathen. I don't know why it takes so much inner work for me to create with my hands and fingers that outer sign of faith and devotion from me to God.

I have learned I am buttoned up too tightly to lift my hands and arms in worship in any way beyond hand clasping and tear wiping. There is a self-consciousness that has stopped me from crossing the bridge to crossing myself, which I think is the same self-imposed caution that stopped me from wading into making a waffle in the extremely popular machine in the hotel dining room. Everyone else seemed to know exactly how to pour in the batter and flip that thing upside down with a flick of the hand. For the two weeks I resided in the Hampton Inn that early fall, I did not attempt to make or eat one single waffle. I smelled other people's waffles instead.

Here in Buechner's book I discovered step-by-step instructions for crossing oneself, even though I don't think that's why he included the scene. He was being writerly in detail, but in it, I found the guidance I sought. I felt safe with the vacuuming lady, so I practiced crossing myself with her in the room. I sensed she wouldn't care one way or the other. If I could do it in front of her, maybe I could do it in front of the whole church. I felt she and I were in some pleasant morning simpatico vibe, as she did her work and I did mine, reading and crossing and recrossing myself in the corner. I decided it was all very peaceful, at least for me.

A loud voice from the nearby front desk broke the reverie. "Do you sell stamps?" a woman asked. The clerk said no. As is often the case, the contents of my bag were spilled out onto the bench on which I sat, and there I saw a package of stamps open, with just one remaining. Queen Elizabeth's tiny stamp face looked up at me with her serene half-smile.

This was my moment to do something generous. I dithered for a second, concerned that later that day I would unexpectedly need a stamp, which has never happened when I am out and about in the larger world. Wanting to cling to my stamp became an even better reason to give it away. I walked to the front desk, pleased with myself, imagining someone in need of a stamp like it was one hundred years ago and all we had to rely on was the mailman.

"I have a stamp you can have," I said.

"One stamp?" the well-dressed woman asked.

"Yes," I answered, holding it out.

"Okay," she said, and took my stamp. "Aren't you sweet."

I returned to my table, already feeling the beginning of post-good-act deflation. *Did she really need my stamp? Won't I need my stamp?*

"Where's the nearest mailbox?" I heard the woman ask then, and my sense of stamplessness expanded and grew. The lady was a bit annoying, really, and it seemed to me she could have figured all this stuff out herself. I missed my stamp.

And so our job then is not to find our resentment delicious, but to be aware of it and how ridiculous we can be, and repent. The giving away of the stamp and the silly post-act feeling both contribute to our life of holiness. We act. We see. We feel gross. We repent, and we can say thank you to God for that small mirror. Thank you for showing me that I am capable of giving away a stamp and regretting it almost immediately. I see I want to be a hero for the hero's sake, and not for your sake. Thank you for the diagnosis. Thank you for the cure.

Once, when I was writing a very tricky article assigned to me about how not to act like a narcissist when you think you might be a narcissist, I interviewed Rod Wilson, a psychologist and author who wrote a book called *Thank You. I'm Sorry. Tell Me More.* He agreed with me that I had been assigned a doozy of an angle. Narcissists don't normally self-diagnose and then immediately strive to get better. But all of us, Rod reminded me, have some narcissistic tendencies lurking within us. How could we not?

Rod offered the reading audience of the *Reader's Digest* a simple exercise to try when you are tempted to put yourself above all others. The exercise, which is a bit like holiness cardio, is making yourself do the opposite of what you are inclined to do. When you start to open your mouth to blab about yourself and your most recent accomplishments, for example, take a pause. Think before you speak, which is what most of us have been hearing from our aunties our entire lives, so this feels like a muscle we know. Instead of sharing your latest and greatest honor, stop and ask other people questions instead. Let them go first. Not only that, but allow them the privilege of finishing their entire sentence, even though you so badly want to cannonball right into the middle of their lake. This is intentionally seeking humility instead of being run over by it.

The opportunities to cultivate humility (and lean into holiness) by doing the opposite of your first and often selfish inclination turn out to be everywhere once you start to pay attention. If you find yourself holding your paper plate first in line at the church buffet, step aside, sir. When you want very badly to go first everywhere and anywhere, practice going last instead, which is what Jesus said to do. If we wait until we feel like going last, we will never be the servant of others that we are asked to be, in so many ways, throughout all of Scripture. "Be devoted to one another in love. Honor one another above yourselves,"[2] Paul wrote to us and the Romans. On purpose, post about other people on social media. Share their books, promotions, accomplishments, and beautiful photos. Point away from yourself and toward others. Pay attention to how that feels. See if you mind. Then repent of that too. Ask Jesus for help. Jesus likes to help us. Eventually, you will be better at this.

In Jesus, we are safe to not talk endlessly about ourselves. We are safe to be quiet in a room full of talking people. We are safe to not have anyone know who we are, even if we are so famous and awesome. We are safe to release and not cling. We are safe to forgive, and to not boast. We can be the ones who don't go on and on about ourselves in all our groups. This is so refreshing to others—like bringing them a glass of water very quietly. We can be the people who don't suck up all the oxygen in the room, but instead carry the light of Jesus in front of us like a tiny lit candle. This is very hard, until it somehow and at some time gets easier. It is impossible for us to be perfect at this and other works of holiness, but we do need to practice. It's all about the practice.

And now, here's the other thing: Secure in God's holiness and believing what God tells us about our own holiness, we can also ask for a glass of water when we need one. Knowing we are worthy, we can tell a friend we need some warm light and someone to stand beside us and care when we're alone or bereft. Bereftness will definitely break in our back window at some point. We must be able to call for help. And because we rejoice with others, we can also share our joy when it shows up, sometimes as much a surprise as sorrow.

When it comes to talking, we can routinely put others first in conversation. And therefore, with even more confidence, we can say, "And now I have something to discuss." But what if you're someone who is overlooked, outtalked, or interrupted often at work or out in the world, like women sometimes are, for example? Perhaps your holy work, for a time at least, is to speak even more and not even less. To fill out your own space a little. Fluff your feathers, friend, because that can also help the other people in the room do a little less talking and more listening. You're doing them a favor, for which they probably will not thank you. But we know we're not in it for the thanks. This is an art and not a science. We can all be better listeners to God and to each other for holy's sake.

Doing the holy opposite, which is the practice of sacrificial love, is everywhere in what Jesus asks of us. Bless those who persecute us. Love our enemies. It would be ideal if we deeply wanted to do those difficult things, but waiting to want to do them is unwise. The wanting takes too long. The waiting could be forever. But even knowing we don't yet want to is a help. Our lack of wanting is a curiosity. We can poke around it a bit and see what we find.

Putting others first in holy humility does not mean we don't also ask ourselves kind questions, probably a little bit later.

Inner Awful Me, we can ask, *why was it so hard not to interrupt that guy?* We can acknowledge that it was difficult to congratulate someone for their silver medal and how much we wanted to bring up our own award. We can be tender with ourselves when we do this. We are not people we should be mean to. That's not the idea.

I first read about the Ignatian practice of *agere contra*—to act against—in Ian Cron's book *The Story of You*. Even though I had never heard the term before, *agere contra* felt deeply familiar, like a cousin I finally got to meet in person at a family reunion. Without knowing its name, I had been trying to practice *agere contra* for years with one besetting sin in particular: that of envy. My practice was tiny but growing. If I was envious of another writer's success, for example, I taught myself to pray for them to be even more successful. I asked God to bless their work and spread their influence. I prayed it out loud, and I asked God to help me mean my prayer.

"Bless them. Help me want them to be blessed. Make them successful. Help me want them to be successful."

Once I mentioned it to another writer friend who told me that was not a problem for her, so I shut up about it for another while. My envy embarrassed me. I was ashamed of it. Ridding myself of it became a little secret pet project of mine. I started to talk about it a bit again at a writers' conference. I confessed it publicly in a talk. Being transparent about my sin—the opposite of hiding—helped me understand that I was not alone, that I wasn't really a green-eyed monster, but instead just a person who sometimes envies. I could confess my sin before God and others. My Spirit-led active resistance against envy had truly taken root.

My *agere contra* practice grew to include pointing to the work of other writers in conversation and online. If I interviewed an author for the podcast I hosted through my day job, I disciplined myself to not mention my own writing life, unless I thought it would make the interview better for the listener, or serve some other practical purpose that made sense. Not serving myself became more enjoyable, and easier.

What took grit then feels just like grace now. *Agere contra* takes determination. It's an act of trust and a surrender of the selfish self to the goodness of God. It is such a relief.

~

No one, except Jesus, has asked us to be holy for them, or to them, or at them. This is a tricky business. In our zeal for feeling we have cracked the mystery of life, we are compelled to share all we have learned and experienced—this amazing grace!—with anyone who will listen.

Generally speaking, this is off-putting. Humility means understanding that we, too, are on a journey, even if we feel we have already arrived because we have walked by the manger and then the cross. We are humble before the mystery of all we do not know, and maybe more significantly, all we don't know that we don't know. A belief in our own spiritual knowingness is unpleasant for ourselves and others.

Humility allows us to say a grateful yes to God's declaration that we are holy in his eyes, and that we have been given that new identity solely through grace. Humility is the air in the tires of our bikes as we set off down the holy-life path. The Bible is full of come-and-go stories. God the Father and Jesus the Son ask people to come, and then tell them to go. Come and become. Go and be different. You have been changed. Go somewhere and make some good changes. Go on! Get out of here!

The path of humility is the path of holiness. The Bible tells us that Jesus, "being in very nature God, did not consider equality with God something to be used to his own advantage; rather, he made himself nothing by taking the very nature of a servant, being made in human likeness. And being found in appearance as a man, he humbled himself by becoming obedient to death—even death on a cross."[3]

We have been freed to not grasp and cling and whine and beg for status. If we are humiliated, which we probably will be at least a few times if we try anything new, or sing too loudly, or experience failure or downward societal sliding in any fashion, we can look to Jesus as the model of humility. He is the best humble company possible. *Agere contra* could come in handy here as well, if we can bring ourselves to whisper, "Thank you for this blessed humiliation," and not be so upset about it. "Thank you for this downfall and all it can teach me."

This is the redemption of the ridiculous. Life does not unfold the way we want it to, usually. We will face an almost continuous parade of events we could not predict, facts we could not know, and events we would never plan. Our hearts will be shattered. If we can say, "Teach me, you miserable thing," we will not waste a single disappointment. There are some losses that are so devastating, it will take us a long time to search for the lessons. That's okay too.

Here is something beautiful that can happen within the communion of humble saints. There will be moments when someone steps aside and we will be the ones invited to go first, and someone will certainly—eventually—listen to our entire sentences. Because someone else is being humble, we will be invited to shine. They will take their Jesus light and position it on the beauty of our own face, and we can stand and shine in that warmth. We will be the last who will be first, every now and then. Our plates will be filled with good things before the best of the potluck vanishes off the tables, and our stories will be heard in their fullness. We will be cared for by others, even as we care. It is true that this can feel rare, but we will know when one of our moments arrives. We can say, "Thank you." It will probably feel humbling in a warm, loving way.

I sat at the table in my in-laws' kitchen. After we were done with a brisk, spirited discussion about how the younger generation doesn't want good wood furniture, we started to chat about humility. Years ago, they had gone on a journey that took them eventually to India, which brought them into the orbit of a man there who served others in a lifelong manner. He was a saint who served people experiencing profound poverty of housing, food, and prospects. One evening over dinner, the man felt moved to pray for some of those friends who had crossed his mind. Maybe he felt bad that he was eating well when they might not have been eating at all.

"I have to pray now," he said to those gathered around the table, and bent his head and summoned Jesus over to the table from where the Lord had been standing in the corner, maybe leaning against the wall. This praying felt completely natural to the rest of the group, and not the least bit showy or awkward, like it might if we did it.

"He was so humble," my mother-in-law said. "He was truly a holy man." So many years later, they remembered his humility first and most of all, along with his unexpected prayer at the dinner table.

I can imagine the man in heaven, being seated in one of the good seats by the maître d'. The man put others first, and so he will be invited to go first someday, or so it seems in the heavenly order of things. It doesn't sound like he would have been thinking about that in the least.

The Bible says that God will exalt the humble.[4] There is a trick to not waiting around for that to happen. But somehow, we must not grasp for it either. When humility itself is viewed as the gift, and not as the shortcut to exaltation, we are finally onto something.

7

BEAUTY

THE RIDEAU STREET CHAPEL, a small churchy space located in the heart of the National Gallery of Canada, welcomes you in with a hush. It feels like a sacred space that quiets you down while lifting you up.

This is a chapel with a dramatic backstory. It is, in fact, a rescue church. After a public outcry against its destruction that included letter-writing campaigns and media conferences held by determined ladies—people on a mission that you don't want to mess with—the chapel was designated an official heritage site. It was dismantled—*deconstructed* is actually the term—and a smaller, more discreet version was pieced together in the National Gallery just blocks away from the original. The Our Lady of the Sacred Heart boarding school, where the chapel originally stood, was demolished.

The chapel's ceiling is vaulted and exceptional and one obvious reason for its salvation. The ceiling brings to mind angels and fans and breezes and God Almighty. For a ceiling—which necessarily cuts off the sky—to create a feeling of air and light and spaciousness is something all church ceilings that stray into magnificence can do. If you could swoop through the air like a little bird, here is where you might try, if you're a person who thinks thoughts like that. All this was designed by Canon Georges Bouillon, a priest who dabbled in architecture in the 1800s.

The ceiling is creamy white with ridged, gilded wooden fan shapes, and a soft blue wash of color that should be called warm ocean. The chapel's stained-glass windows are not nearly as fancy. They are simply a bright, clear offering of pinks, blues, reds, and greens. There are no Bible story images of men pulling in nets full of fish or holy babies with their mothers. The colors are their own story. "I am red, looking surprisingly pleasing right next to pink. Here is clear blue. Green can be so fresh and surprising. Enjoy us." Statues of saints and angels stand watch, a bit sternly, as you sit and listen.

You listen to *Spem in alium*, by sixteenth-century English composer Thomas Tallis. Written for eight choirs of five voices each, the piece is meant to be sung with the audience sitting smack-dab in the middle of the choirs circled around them. Sound artist Janet Cardiff recreated that experience by recording the Salisbury Cathedral Choir on forty different microphones in a medieval hall, and we get to listen to it through forty speakers spaced out around the perimeter of Rideau Chapel. "I have never put my hope in any other but in thee, God of Israel" spills out in mysterious, majestic Latin from each speaker and fills this small, tenderly saved, and carefully reconstructed space. The music, written for worship—and maybe a little showing off by Tallis, but that is understandable—is so skillfully sung and artfully arranged and carefully spaced out around the chapel, you can't help but feel you are sitting exactly within *Spem in alium*, beside its very heart. And not just that, but that you yourself, with all your business and bluster and ambitions and heartache and joy, are present in the music and within the Latin floating through the air.

But that's not even the best part. If you sit through this whole rendering of *Spem in alium*, you will reach a pause in the singing, which is the intermission and a break for the singers. Wonderfully, the artist kept the microphones on and the recording going. The singers chuckle and practice their scales. They chat. There's an abundance of throat clearing, a resting up and resetting for the next part. That the artist included this humanity in what otherwise feels like a perfect blending of forty angelic voices into one velvet cloth is an earthy delight. Real people with car loans and appointments and tickles in their throats made this worshipful beauty. They received an amazing gift they have worked to refine and improve, creating a kind of beauty that shows us who sit and listen that there *is* such beauty, that it exists and comes from God and points to God and is because of God. We are capable of beauty. This fact is so beautiful in itself. It is reason enough to sit there all day and soak. It reminds us of God. That is the constant invitation of that which is beautiful.

⁓

Beauty is so hopeful and, also, slows time down. Beauty shares that with holiness: its inherent hope and also its pace. When we make things beautiful, or pause to notice beauty already existing, it is a rebellion of optimism against all the long, ordinary moments and things, and certainly that which is ugly in and of the world. Noticing beauty is a belief in now, and in five minutes from now.

Things that are beautiful—like the perfect puff of a cloud against a blue sky, or a masterful painting of a perfect puff of a cloud against a blue sky, for example—invite us to slow down to notice. Things shouldn't be so rushed. We can stand still and gaze. We pause and notice when a dragonfly lands on our head, as we should. One landed on my head once as Brent and I bobbed in a lake, chatting, and my husband turned to me and said, "A dragonfly bit me once, and I knew it was an error." It was such a particular thing to remember and such an oddly beautiful thing to say. His words were a poem to me, and I said them over and over in my head the entire boat ride home so I could write them down on the back of an advertisement for a place called Molly's Farm. That piece of paper is now worn and soft from folding and being tucked into the pages of books. Now it's stuck on the wall near where I often work, in my kitchen. I wanted to remember the beauty of his wonder.

Wonder allows us to forgive dragonflies. The moment and the mindfulness required to notice that something is beautiful slows us down in a way that is good for us and for the world, and for our hearts. That is the surprise of both natural and created beauty, which remind us that God is real, that God is holy, and that God is beautiful. Beauty points us away from ourselves and toward beauty's original maker, who is God. God combined ingredients and made daffodils and mud, the ocean and the butterflies. God made you and me. God makes all things beautiful. God is the maker of all makers, the God of make-dom, and all beauty points back to God and those original moments of making.

We make because God first made us. Anything beautiful we make is a reflection of the beautiful work of God, and of God's heart, which is beautiful. Beautiful things that are crafted with care and skill by us, and don't just drop hovering out of the sky like a dragonfly, can take years of training (but not always). Usually, there is intention and design. We have decided to try to make something lovely. There's been a decision to spend time, effort, and energy, all for the sake of beauty and often for little else. This decision to create also reflects God's way of creation, the orderly path God took, the millions of decisions we believe God made to do such a masterful work.

Paying too much attention to beautiful things or trying to make something beautiful can feel like a waste of time or effort to some people who are trying to be especially holy in a certain way, perhaps, but it's not a waste. Look at the hummingbird hanging in the air like a tiny helicopter, whirring through space searching for syrup. Such an intricate and hardworking bird, with its tiny bones and racing wings—and, one can only assume, its racing heart—cannot help but point us to heaven and lead us into contemplation of the endlessly creative Creator. Beauty matters to God. Also, Jesus was clearly a bird guy. "Look at the birds of the air; they do not sow or reap or store away in barns, and yet your heavenly Father feeds them. Are you not much more valuable than they?" he asks us in Matthew.[1] And remember, we will soar on wings like eagles in Isaiah, and God sends us out like innocent doves.[2] Beauty and birds—thousands upon thousands of different species in the world—are woven into creation, available at every turn and on branches that are themselves like sculptures if we can see them that way, reminding us to be mindful and to notice. Beauty is everywhere.

"Did you hear the birds this morning?" Brent asked so often that now it is a line in our family liturgy. We comment regularly about birdsong, with a smile. Their songs give us hope that winter will come to an end someday, as it always does. Spring will softly arrive.

Beautiful things and places, like baked bread or Rideau Street Chapel, or the way tulip petals drift down and make a little silky pile at the base of the vase, please us, and they help us to experience the gratitude that is part of the call and invitation of holiness. Beauty reminds us of God, and of how good it is to be here right now, in this place, looking at that canyon or this painting.

One day I walked with my dog down the road, and I could feel the sunshine on my shoulders. They were warmed by the sun in a way that made me feel the sun was in the sky on that day for shoulder-warming purposes alone, and I was happy to be in the sun with everyone else. I made my way up Bank Street, a long road that, depending on the section, means you are in nice Ottawa, or else in not-so-nice Ottawa. We live in not-so-nice Ottawa, so that's the part of Bank where the sun most often shines on me. The area is not beautiful in any kind of traditional way. Cannabis shops sprout like weeds in contrast to the fine shops on Nice Bank, like the haberdashery where one Christmas I bought Brent a rabbit hat that stood too high on his head and made us all laugh out loud. He exchanged it for another big hat, which he wore at an increasingly jaunty angle that, although embarrassing, was endearing. I smiled when I saw it. Even the jauntiness of a hat can be beautiful, for all it reveals.

On the day the sun walked above me up my part of Bank, my elderly dog walked behind me. I was aware of his heavy weight at the end of the leash, which I gently pulled. An equally elderly man, in dog and human years both, rode by me in the opposite direction on his not-at-all-nice bike. His sideburns framed his face in the lamb-chop style. He wore a faded ball cap, and smoke from the cigarette he held between his lips trailed up to his eyes, which met mine, as if we were in an old western. Some understanding passed between us. Maybe it was about the sunny day and the faithfulness of an old dog, and the oldness of him, too, and the way he smoked while cycling. We were two strangers joined together for just a second on a shared mission of noticing. The day got even better, and it did feel holy; not quite like a chapel, but almost.

We know holiness when we feel it. And when we feel holiness, we know it. Those moments are a gift that can sustain us on our journey. We might even have chills running down our spine, or we might feel a flush of warmth that reminds us we are closer than we think to God, the source of all holiness, the original of all holiness, from whom all holiness flows. Beauty can be objectively helpful in appreciating holiness, but it can also move us so deeply that we feel it in a way that can sustain us for a little while.

After I had my holy feeling with the man on the bike, I passed a woman wearing purple pants. "I like your pants!" I called out. I sensed her discomfort. I had miscalculated my charm. But if I had purple pants, I'd like to hear about their beauty from someone. One should expect it. We can be lavish with each other and remind the people we love and the people we pass that they are beautiful, and that they remind us of holiness because of it.

I passed grandparents—they just had to be—walking across a patch of grass to a first-floor apartment window, calling out, "Stella! You're not Stella!" And then, "There you are, Stella!" I imagined a child inside running to the window (but maybe it was a cat) and the beautiful lightness of inner joy we feel when someone we love shows up and is so overjoyed to see us. They behold us even if just through a window and say our name as if we were a treat. You are a treat. God is always so glad to see you. We are fortunate because of that. That is also beauty lived out, as if we ourselves were a painting. You are a painting.

God makes us beautiful with love and enables us to create beauty in our lives and hearts and with our hands and with our mouths. Creating is a way of loving God and others. Making anything— the bread itself or the bowl in which the warm yeast will burst into its new life—is an exertion of holiness that springs best and most freely from our own belovedness and the assurance that God sees us as holy and beautiful.

The joy we feel in response to God's love and creativity can make us more generous with ourselves and others, and with how we move and how we are in the world, and not just with how we make or take in beauty. To be made beautiful in God's love, to be reassembled by God's maker hands, is to be the clay in the Potter's hands, like Scripture says.[3] There is no better way to be smoothed and shaped, to be remade and reimagined, to be made beautiful and holy.

On the radio once, as I was driving down the highway through Quebec, I heard an accomplished pianist tell a story about how he had been listening to a symphony on the radio and admired the arrangement and the skill of the players. As he listened to the orchestra, he found himself wishing he could play so smoothly and so free of fumbles. When the piece ended, the pianist was shocked and then delighted to learn it had been his very own orchestra playing. He himself had been playing in the recorded piece he had admired. It was his own skill and the skill of his playing partners he had accidentally enjoyed.

The pianist, whose name was James, said that musicians usually hear only what they do wrong, and that they are acutely aware of the dozens of little mistakes they might make while playing, which we ordinary listeners would probably never hear. They are their own harshest critics, like we all can be. Just look at a photo of yourself and see how you feel. But in hearing his orchestra play without realizing that there he was in the middle of it all, James allowed himself to relax and acknowledge and appreciate even a little bit his own skill in a way he never would have otherwise. He offered himself an accidental grace. He had given himself a tiny round of applause without knowing it.

There was so much to admire in this story. The skill of the pianist, and his humility, of course. The years of practicing and the joy and anguish of performing, and the way the artist was so quick to appreciate others, and was surprised and embarrassed, yet pleased, when he accidentally admired his own orchestra's piece. For a moment, he saw that he did beautiful work.

Maybe we are like this with holiness, too. We can more easily see it in others, and not in ourselves, because that, appropriately, feels weird. When we see the beauty of holiness in each other, maybe we need to say that out loud, to encourage one other. "I like your purple pants," we can say. "Keep going. You are on the right track. Yes, that's you on the piano, and you are playing so well. Sometimes I can glimpse you living out of and into your holiness wonderfully." I wonder why we don't tell each other these things more often. That we are beautiful and holy. I would find that very encouraging.

Sometimes, after all, we must be positioning ourselves well into the life of Christ. We can't always be completely missing the mark, because that would eventually call into question the ability of the Potter, I think. Sometimes we are abiding well. Some days we are making things more beautiful and being made a little more beautiful ourselves. Our lives might not often be *Spem in alium*, but because of who God is, we will be music in the world. We can remind each other of that, occasionally. I'm certain that no one will get too big for their britches if we whisper in their ear every now and then that they have been made both holy and beautiful, and we can see it so clearly.

At the end of the radio show in which James the pianist shared how he had unwittingly enjoyed his own music, he wrapped up in this way (I wrote it down because it was so refreshing): "I hope you've enjoyed these concerto recordings. These are some of my favorites. As a matter of fact, I love them so much I think I'm going to have to go home and listen to some of them again." Yes.

⌒

When people think of beauty and holiness, they might think of paint and pewter and other raw ingredients blended together by skilled hands to create the art of our faith. Art can present beauty and holiness on a canvas or in macrame or clay and tell us something we might be missing about God and the world. Art can also slow us down and make us hopeful, like holiness and beauty do.

We purchased our first piece of art back at Regent College in the '90s, from their art gallery. Brent was a seminary student and I was a hard worker. We often ran out of money, but that was all part of it. We ate at a restaurant with endless french fry refills and shamelessly ate fries off one shared plate until we could eat no more, wondering if the waitress disliked us as much as it felt.

I asked my husband if he recalled what we paid for the watercolor hanging in our kitchen, painted by a student. It is of a yellow coffee cup passing between two hands. There's a caption penciled at the bottom: . . . *more coffee? Oh yes!*

"Eighty dollars," Brent answered. We would have weighed that cost in our minds. There would have been more prudent ways to spend what was hard-earned. There would have been a shot of pleasure at making a married-couple purchase that was not a plate of fries or winter tires or milk and eggs, but art instead, made by hand and so pleasingly composed and rendered. It was valuable just for being beautiful.

I remember what that piece articulated for us back then, just starting out. We wanted to practice hospitality. "More coffee?" "Oh yes!"

When we left our first parish postings in northern Saskatchewan, the two churches Brent served gave us an envelope with $500 cash. The envelope was heavy in my hand and so reassured me. We bought *Chepwa Point* by Glenn Veeman and *Open Country* by Terry Lindsay, instead of the gas for our car the churches probably intended. The paintings reminded us of wild and open things and places, and the blues and greens of the prairies. They marked a time and place, and made our space more beautiful.

"Who's the artist?" people occasionally ask when they come into our house for the first time. I always felt I needed to explain why we would waste money on beauty. I do that less now, because I care less what other people think. I value beauty too much to feel bad about it. This comes with age and one too many conversations that feel unnecessary.

In the Bible, art making is directed by God, even down to the details sometimes. Art makes holy space even more beautiful. Old Testament linen is finely woven, clasps are golden, curtains are carefully designed with blue, purple, and scarlet thread, exactly on purpose. God requested that. Beauty matters. The artists through their art point to the Artist who came first, the One about whom the preacher speaks and the writer writes.

In two churches, Brent created gallery space and made an art gallery. Church walls, normally hung with defibrillators and evacuation directions or, often, nothing at all, became gallery walls. It was such a simple idea. I don't know what it was like for the artists, but I know it was wonderful for the rest of us. To pause at and ponder a painting. To read the little cards that guided and explained. Clustered together, each painting was like a chapter of a book, leading one to another and hinting at a bigger, more complete story.

People can look, and linger, and gaze. To gaze is good.

⌒

When I was a girl, I sat for one long morning at an outdoor market behind a table full of earrings made from bright, plastic buttons. I don't know how I came up with this idea, or why I thought it was a good one, but I glued earring backs to dozens of sets of buttons. One Saturday my father drove me to the Sackville flea market. I don't remember if I sold even a single set, but I do remember I retired from jewelry making that very day, just past noon.

Humbled? Certainly. Deterred? Not at all. I liked to make things.

I enrolled in a stained glass–making course and discovered I wasn't a cut-things-in-a-straight-line kind of artist. I moved on and moved to Vancouver. There, I abandoned soapmaking when I stumbled upon what lye feels like splashed on the soft flesh of the inner arm. Papermaking was wet and wonderful, but my paper was always lumpy.

Then I stumbled on a magazine for "Canadian crafters" in a hobby store I wandered through, searching for my next big thing. I had been writing for a few years by then, short pieces for small papers in tiny places, which I think is how writers should start, growing good slowly. I wove the threads of my misadventures together into a piece called "Confessions of a Failed Crafter," and I made it onto the cover.

"Goodbye, Crafting!" I said, maybe forever. "Bon voyage!" Crafting yelled back, and slammed the door behind me.

In writing, I discovered my clay, my paints, and my mandolin. Writing would be my art and my craft, and reading would be one way I would move myself into beauty and know a little more deeply the creative beauty-making side of God, maker of heaven and earth, the sea and all the things in them, as the psalmist reminds us.[4]

The very act of creating—the journey to the finished thing—matters as much as the thing itself, whether it's a book or weird button earrings. Beauty points us to God, but so does the making of handmade beauty. Making itself has an important weight and is worthy of our trust. If we find something we particularly love to make, we will do it over and over again and trust the process that moves us from nothing to something. When we do the same thing over and over again, we are training ourselves, and when a long time has passed, we find we will likely be better. Practice makes better. Holiness is slowly like this. Over the long arc of our story, we will grow closer to who God created us to be, our truest holy selves.

People who try to make beautiful things love to learn about how other people try to make beautiful things. We are curious about training and technique, failures and flops, and how someone makes what they make so well. I read *Daily Rituals: How Artists Work* by Mason Currey and loved the glimpses into the creative working lives of artists of all kinds. It is about how artists do what they do.

Alice Munro, my beloved Canadian short-story artist, wrote, at the beginning at least, during her children's nap times, and then later when they were in school. Thomas Mann was always in his study by nine o'clock in the morning, where he wrote undisturbed until noon. Choreographer George Balanchine planned and created while he ironed his clothing almost daily. Ironing was a part of his process. He trusted the ironing. All the processes of highly creative and accomplished writers, artists, musicians, and super-smart math people are different, as they all discover how to do good work well within the possibilities of their own lives. And then they hit repeat (and tweak occasionally, of course).

The process I trust is to read, think, walk, read, walk, despair, write, regret, and revise again and again and again. Revision is everything. I finish my piece, then I send it to my editor, am weird right away and go into the sent folder to read the email, see a ridiculous error, and email the editor again almost immediately.

This process works for me, again and again. I know it and I trust it, although there are parts of it that I always hate. If I don't abandon the process, I know that when I start with reading, I will finish by emailing my editor twice in a row. I believe in this.

Making handmade beauty is not about being perfect—it's about messy, wonderful creating leading to a new creation. It's process and trust and courage. Every year my parents kneel down on the green grass and pick 250 dandelions, which they snip and boil into four cups of dandelion syrup, which they decant into tiny mason jars like thick, runny gold. "It's all natural except for the two cups of sugar in it," my father says, and laughs. It's such a wonderful waste of time. When I am in my eighties, I hope I have time like that on my hands as well as knees that allow it, and I hope I use my time, my hands, and my knees to make a tiny amount of syrup from the flowers that I will pick and count. Making is sinking our fingers into the soil and our brushes into the paint. It is time spent well in process. It's the stirring before the stopping.

Being holy is not about being perfect either. Worship is also about process for us. When we step into church and offer our selves—our souls and bodies—in the sacred sentences of worship, which we will eventually know by heart if we go often and long enough, this is a deep relinquishment of trying to be our best. We enfold ourselves into the worship. We are invited, even there, to trust the process. We show up. Showing up for beauty and worship and holiness is where we begin.

Beauty and holiness, and beauty in holiness, are not necessarily productive in the way we normally consider productivity. That's one of the things that make them not make practical sense. Every Sunday at church, someone stands up from their pew and comes down front to lead the prayers of the people. Together, each week, we offer this same petition: "We pray for wars to cease in all the world." What a ridiculous prayer. The world feels like it is mostly on fire, mostly all the time. But still we boldly ask, and we try to believe it is possible that someday all wars will cease in all the world. It is faithful to ask. It's our task to ask, because that is what we deeply want and what the world needs, and surely what God also desires.

The odds are against this and many other things, but nevertheless we pray. We ask, and sometimes we plead. And then, nevertheless, we paint and sculpt and dance. Beauty and holiness don't always make sense. They are radical in that way. Beauty often brings only itself to the party. It just is, because God made it somehow spectacular; or some under-maker made it because Maker God made us to want to do that. We are made to make. God made us thirsty for beauty and able to create it. God made us holy and able to live that way, even when it all feels highly unlikely.

Jesus is in Bethany, reclining at the table of a friend, when a woman, now famous forever because of her holy wastefulness, arrives with her jar of perfume and stirs the pot. "As she stood behind him at his feet weeping, she began to wet his feet with her tears. Then she wiped them with her hair, kissed them and poured perfume on them," reported Luke.[5] The other diners are scandalized, and we can understand how this could make us all very uncomfortable. That feeling only deepens when Jesus forgives her sins and sends her away to a new life. "Your faith has saved you," he says in Luke 7:50. "Go in peace." She is a love lavisher and a perfume waster, and now a woman restored and redeemed. Jesus clearly appreciated her over-the-top, over-the-foot gesture and being loved in this way, with the devotion of long hair, the tender cleansing and kissing of feet, and perfume that only served the purpose of worship and anointing.

Jesus said to his friends that what the woman did was a beautiful thing.[6] And what you have done is a beautiful thing, Jesus will someday say to you and to me.

8

CHURCH

"DANCE YOURSELF AWAKE" was the first item on the
Saturday morning schedule of a spiritual retreat I attended with
a few other women from my church. The weekend getaway was
held on the grounds of a Christian camp on a lake not far from
our city. The main building of the camp was built on a hill with
a gentle slope down to the lake and a firepit, and to the small
gym where Dance Yourself Awake was scheduled for eight o'clock
in the morning.

I texted my daughter, a camp veteran, and asked for courage.
I don't know what Dance Yourself Awake actually is, I wrote.

Go, Mom, she answered. *Be brave. No one is there watching you.*

I went. Worship music played from a portable stereo at the
front of the room. The leader welcomed us and asked us to spread

out, find our spot, and dance in worship all by ourselves but also there together in the gym. I wanted to flee but decided to try. I shuffled from foot to foot and flapped my hands around. I moved, as rhythmically as possible, backward from the spot I had naively chosen in the center of the gymnasium toward the safety of the rear wall. There I stood and swayed under a basketball net, still feeling silly. I watched some of the other women dancing, their arms swept upward to heaven and their whole bodies bowing low. It was astonishing to me how freely they moved. It was an impromptu and, if I'm to be completely honest, not very good church ballet. I tried not to stare. I knew that I could not dance myself awake in this manner. I simply could not manage this activity asked of me.

I edged to my escape, along the wall toward the door that stretched so far away in the gym that seemed to have grown bigger. I discovered Laurie from my church, standing as still as a frightened deer.

"Is it okay for us to leave?" she whispered.

"Yes," I said, and we walked back up the hill to the dining hall and found coffee.

All the women there, those who were free to dance and we who were free to leave, loved Jesus. Still, we found each other weird. The church itself is deeply weird, unlike anything else most of us have ever seen or experienced. The church combines people as different from one to another as they can be, or it should and could when it's healthy and diverse. We are a strange soup. We share the reality of having been made holy because of who God is and what Jesus did, and then welcomed into the body of Christ, where we stumble upon each other. We are made holy alone and then live holy together, or we try.

We are people who have allowed ourselves to be pulled into this life raft that stretches through history and around the world. Once we were drowning, and now we sit in this boat, bobbing on the waves of grace. We are all in the same boat, just like our neighbor Mary said about the grief that was present at our neighborhood Advent party.

Holiness is and holiness does, and that is true of the church as well. The church is the people, yes, we all know that. But church is also the actual activity that usually, but not always, plays out on Sunday mornings. Church services are a human endeavor for a holy purpose. We are pilgrims together, walking alongside people with whom we might never choose to share even a cup of coffee on a Monday morning, let alone an intense lifelong journey toward the One who beckons us forward. But there we are together, rushing in late and sneaking out early, moving deeper into holiness and eventually into heaven.

We will spend eternity with people that we wouldn't choose to go bowling with.

Church can be a thorn in our side and a pain in our behind. It is also balm and beauty. A lot happens at church.

⁓

"God is a powerful promise keeper," said Shane, an intern at our parish. It was his turn to preach. It wasn't a fancy sermon. Shane, who served as chaplain at city hall during the week, popping in and out of the city jail to visit with people, didn't include even one personal story, something I have always encouraged Brent to do.

"People want to hear about your experiences," I've told him, which I guess may not always have been true.

On that day there were no anecdotes in Shane's preaching, and he didn't quote a single scholar or writer. It was a shorter sermon than usual because it was summer. The church promised the parents that for one month the service would be shorter and sweeter because there wasn't a Sunday school to which they could send their squirming, sometimes squealing children.

"God is your shield," Shane said softly. "He will keep his promises, and he is there for you." There were no dramatic pauses, or antics of any kind. Shane calmly read out loud what we collectively were trying to believe. He reminded us of how much we are loved, and how God showed us that love, and what that meant for our lives. There wasn't really anything new to learn, unless you were hearing the gospel for the first time, which, looking around the congregation as I usually do during the service, felt unlikely. I knew almost everyone there that day.

For most of us, what Shane preached were old, true things we needed to hear once again, the fabulous and ordinary things of our faith. At church, almost every week, we learn old things again, and that helps keep making us new. We help each other believe. Sometimes when we feel we can hardly believe anything, we can believe in the belief of the preacher, or the friend we stand beside at the coffeepot. When we just don't think we can do what Jesus would do, we can think about what very faithful-seeming Anne would do, and we can start there. We need each other. Holiness happens alone, but also, very importantly, together. Holiness is relational, and we are helped by being with people who are also trying to believe and remember that they are holy and called to live holy lives.

Part of the work of church is to remind us that we are tenderly and personally loved, and that although this is true, it is also not about us, and we don't live this life alone. We come in through the doors once a week, after the rushing and maybe some ironing or steaming and complaining, to hear again that it's all about God, and it's about understanding and worshiping God in community, together. Church is where we remember that holiness is a gift. We are reoriented, every time, back toward the God who makes ordinary things and ordinary people like us holy. Water and words, bread and wine, you and me—all this ordinary matter transformed because of God's grace, which makes all things new.

The standing and the sitting, the praying and the preaching, the sitting quietly and the wrestling with our own thoughts are all part of the exercise of worship that happens at church. Once during the prayers of the people, I mused inwardly about how the actress Julia Roberts had kept her marriage together for so long. *What are other people thinking about?* I wondered. I worried about my inattention to the service and my strange interest in Julia Roberts. Then I prayed for the actress who had popped into my roaming mind, because she was alive in my thoughts there at church whether I wanted her to be or not, and the prayer felt redemptive of my wandering mind. Later, I tried not to write a grocery list.

This is how we bring our mess, and how we tidy up together. It is okay to be exactly who we are, and it is also good and right to move a little closer to who God created us to be. To do what God is asking of us, separately and together.

In our church, which skews formal with a huge dash of warmth, the Gospel lesson is read out loud in the middle of the service from the middle of the center aisle on the red rug that stretches from one end of the church to the other, nave to chancel. The congregation stands for the reading, if we are able, and we turn ourselves to face the reader. This listening is a physical and spiritual act, and we know the two almost always hold each other's hands. The reader is accompanied by a small group of friends, usually kids dressed in choir-like gowns holding lit candles placed in tall holders lifted high. Another youth carries a cross and leads the group from the front of the building to the center of the middle aisle, like a parade marshal.

"The Gospel of Christ," the reader says, hoisting the Bible up for all to see.

"Glory to you, Lord Jesus Christ," the people respond, and then all the inadequate but deeply beloved saints stand in this church-sized circle and try to pay attention to the words of Jesus. It feels fancy, with the candles and gowns and singing of a verse or two of a song as the group processes up the aisle to read and back to the front when they are done. It might seem a bit uptight, and it's awkward if you find yourself accidentally staring into the eyes of another parishioner listening on the other side of the circle. You might want to give a little wave, and if you do, you wish you hadn't.

The first time you experience this kind of Gospel reading, it can remind you of times when you didn't know which fork to use. *Why does this need to be so formal?* But this stiff linen napkin of a reading, folded just so on a special plate, can remind us that God is the originator and bestower of the holiness of every ordinary thing or person that can be transformed, including us. Even if the church we attend is as casual as a picnic, there are moments when the otherness of worship breaks through and we know we are in the presence of holiness. Sometimes it is appropriate for that to take our breath away. God is the holy other, and so we are put in our place in a comfortable and reassuring way. Our spirits can be snug in this right ordering of relationship. We are reminded also that the church itself is holy, and that it really is quite something to be told we are holy too, no matter how we feel about it on that very morning.

That summer morning in our fancy, formal service, after Shane preached, the great commandment was then read out loud, as part of the liturgy: "'Love the Lord your God with all your heart and with all your soul and with all your mind.' This is the first and greatest commandment. And the second is like it: 'Love your neighbor as yourself.' All the Law and the Prophets hang on these two commandments."[1] Immediately following that reading, knowing well the far corners of our hearts and wildness of our minds, we throw ourselves at the feet of God by saying: "Christ, have mercy." And then "Lord, have mercy." These words show that we know fully that we will fall short. We know it will be tough to act holy as we are holy in this most basic way of loving God with all our heart and all our soul and then loving our neighbors as ourselves. We need mercy. Church makes us lovers of mercy, if we are listening.

Brent offered the benediction. "As you leave," he said, "remember, it's not just back to normal." Then we took Shane and his wife, Ingrid, out to lunch. Brent and Shane wore their white collars and their black clerical shirts, and people in the restaurant looked at them as if they were aliens landed from another planet. That was fine.

The church is called the communion of the saints. We are saints, and we are communing. We spend our lives sinking into our sainthood, trying to accept it for ourselves and believe the same of others. Our discomfort and difficulty in believing we are saints is quite normal. It's also hard to believe it of others sometimes, although depending on the day and our mood, we might be tricked into thinking we are way better or way worse than the others around us.

We know ourselves and our own lives best, no matter what we think we know about the others straggling into the parking lot.

On the inside we are cranky, envious, irritated, selfish, critical, insecure, impatient, and so much more. We are prone to loathe others and ourselves, and this is even after we have been baptized holy. That list of the fruit of the Spirit—love, joy, peace, patience, kindness, goodness, faithfulness, gentleness, and self-control—can feel like an inventory of the ways we have not grown instead of a picture of what is possible. Fruit is aspirational. Holy people are the ones who dance themselves awake, we are tempted to think. The rest of us go for coffee.

We are ragged saints, each one of us. The worse we feel on a given day or week, the less we might believe we can bear our status as saint and our identity as holy. Brokenness feels more comfortable to discuss. It's easier to share how we have not grown than how we have changed because of God's grace, even incrementally, as it moves like a caterpillar across the surface of our lives. Holiness sounds like a foreign country on the other side of the world instead of the ground we are directly standing on, right beneath our feet, and which we are invited to explore, here, in this church.

Here, we can say together that we have failed and that we have been forgiven. We are restored. We may enter feeling old and burdened, but inside those walls we are reminded that we are made new, and we are lifted by a light breeze. We remember that we have seen it all and we have seen nothing yet. We each know our beginning, but we have no idea about our end and all that will be required of us, about what will be taken and what will be given. At church we are reminded every single week that no matter what goes wrong, there is a center where Jesus stands, warm and risen. That is the precious belief and relief of our faith.

At church, we are exhorted, challenged, and comforted in the ways of holiness. We are tutored in its means and methods. We are reminded that we really are the very people we think we are not, which are saints. No one wants to go to church all the time. But it's good to try to go, especially when we don't want to. *Agere contra* your way out of your house and to church. At least some of the time you will be glad you went.

We are part of an amazing body that includes you and me and maybe some of your most annoying cousins, Peter confessing to Jesus that he loves him and that, yes, he will certainly feed his sheep, and Mary, who heard Jesus call her by name the morning he revealed himself to be resurrected. The family we belong to includes Augustine of Hippo along with Myrtle from our church, who makes an extraordinarily spicy homemade hot sauce for anyone who wants it. We are included, and we belong. We matter in this body, and we matter to it. We belong here even though sometimes we don't think that at all. We can't sever the spiritual umbilical cord that connects us to this mystical, beautiful body of Christ, even if we stop going to church. "If the foot says, 'I am not a part of the body because I am not a hand,' that does not make it any less a part of the body,'" writes Paul, to us and to the Corinthians.[2] We now belong to something so much bigger and more beautiful than our own human lives. We grow best when we are together and turned toward Jesus, no matter how annoying it can all be.

⁓

"I will disappoint you," Brent has warned every church that has called him to be their pastor. He knew they were only seeing the best version of himself on a résumé, or hearing his best sermon in the clips he sent. They were seeing their own hope for their church. There he was in front of the selection committee with a fresh haircut and a clean clerical shirt, never as if he had rolled right out of bed, rumpled and worn. He hadn't let them down yet, but he warned them that he might and likely would. Pastors and ministers always do, I think. They are mere mortal flesh, like the rest of us, just with a slightly different role than most of us.

Sometimes people hope, understandably, that the pastor will grow the church into the biggest one in town and that this church will finally be the one that holds the best Vacation Bible School. People think the minister has a recipe for holiness that they will bake into a pie and serve their congregation with ice cream, easy and delicious. They think the pastor always believes more and behaves better than everyone else, and then along comes one who behaves worse, who makes everyone look horrible. So many lives of pastors and ministry leaders have been deeply and painfully reproachable, the opposite of what Paul wrote in 1 Timothy: that a church leader's life must be "above reproach."[3]

The Book of Common Prayer ordination service does not mince words: "How weighty is this Office" to which the ordinands are called, it says. "Remember how great is this treasure committed to your charge," and the treasure is the church that is the body and the bodies that are the church.

"If the church, or any of her members, is hurt or hindered by your negligence, you must know both the gravity of your fault and the grievous judgment that will result."

Sober and relentless, the ordination service continues. "Will you be diligent to frame and fashion your own life, according to the doctrine of Christ, and to make yourself a wholesome example and pattern to the flock of Christ?"[4] *Wholesome* is an antique of a word; uncomfortable when it's applied to a person and not a sandwich. Pastors vow to be as wholesome as thick, grainy bread in a kitchen filled with light. They vow to not do unholy things but lead in the way of holiness when they are invited to do so, and they promise not to hurt other people. Pastors say they will be especially and predictably holy, and point others toward that warm light.

Pastors who meet in coffee shops with people who think they want to be pastors almost always say, "If you can do anything else, do anything else instead." It can be a difficult life. Expectations are long. Money is short. Your kids will feel the weight, and so will your spouse. No one can predict just how hard it will be, but the holiness part of the clerical life is clear from the beginning. No one can say they didn't think they would have to try to be holy, and to encourage others to do the same. They vowed to do this hard and beautiful work. They stepped into this lonely office and switched on the light.

When pastors act in the exact opposite way from the way of holiness, they remind us that anyone is capable of anything. Their hearts are as deceitful as anyone else's. This shouldn't come as a surprise, really, but it always does. We see again that they are only badly human. If we are honest, we understand that we also are capable of living a life that looks outwardly holy but is not that, in case we thought differently. But when pastors don't choose holy, they leave a big mess in the living room.

When leaders fall and pastors fail in the spectacular ways they sometimes do, a thick fog sinks over the church. When a pastor or a priest breaks their vows and does things that are undeniably unholy, they break other people's hearts. They do such damage. People leave the church in droves, and we can see why this is so.

A lot of people don't trust pastors now because of the ones who did not live into and act out of their holiness, those who set their commitment to their holiness down like baggage at the airport and walked away. Their reasons—tired, lonely, tempted, misunderstood, overworked, merely human, always kind of a jerk—don't change the consequences. The *why* hardly matters, although the church should always spend some time trying to find an answer, or help the pastor find a few. But if your "Why?" gets answered in this and other matters of life, you are especially fortunate.

We in the church fail each other, and the church fails itself. It's always been disappointing in some way, since its very first day. "We will disappoint each other," we should all turn to each other and say, maybe weekly. That's what the letters in the New Testament seem to be about, how much help we need to do church and life together well. How we are glory and guck, all together.

⌐

On a quiet midweek afternoon, standing there with my dog, I was blessed by an old woman who lived alone in her room at a local senior residence. She was the widow of a minister, so we had the clergy life in common, along with a nagging sense of almost continually missing the mark, which amused us to chat about. One day I told her I was moving, and I wouldn't be able to visit her anymore as a volunteer therapy-dog team, along with Dewey. So Millicent raised her cardigan-clad arm and blessed me from where she sat in the corner. She raised her arm slowly, slowly, moving it up and then down, and then made a cross, gently, gently, so that it almost hung in the air in front of me. I felt the holy. A few years later, when I received word from her daughter that Millicent had died, I could still close my eyes and feel the shape of that moment, warm and full in front of me.

We know when we are on holy ground, whether we're standing on a rug in an old lady's apartment or on a pub floor tacky with spilled beer. We recognize holiness coming our way from someone else as it unfolds and wraps around our shoulders.

The day of Millicent's blessing I broke into a light jog, which I rarely ever do, to make it home before I forgot any details. At the time I was writing a book about being a minister's wife, and I knew I had been blessed in a godly way, yes, but also blessed as a writer with a scene for my work. Writers are like that. We're hungry hounds. I wrote about Millicent and her raised arm and the connection I felt to her and God. She blessed me. I was blessed. I held the holy in my cupped and grateful hands.

Months passed. I chose that passage to read to my writing class, who met one night for the purpose of reading out loud to each other in a packed pub. Because I am a chicken, I waited until the end to do my reading, when the crowd's attention had firmly turned toward platters of poutine and pitchers of cold beer.

I blathered on about Millicent and me, then set the microphone down on the chair for the next sucker. I made my way through the crowded pub toward the door and the warm summer air. I couldn't wait to breathe in the relief of being done. A woman from my class, the same one who had been kind to me and asked me to tour her through our wedding chapel, stepped out of the shadows and grabbed my arm.

"Bless me," she said. "Bless me like that woman blessed you."

And so I did, of course. "The Lord bless you and keep you," I spoke into her ear. "The Lord make his face shine upon you and give you peace. Amen." And I gave her a little squeeze.

Blessed are those who stand in a pub late at night, longing for a blessing and finding the courage to ask. They will be blessed.

We churchy people take blessings for granted. We fling them around as if they were ordinary. We forget how extraordinary it is to speak holiness and love over another human. Blessings are a burst of God's love, attention, and intentions to us and for us, through us and with us. A blessing is a reminder of who God is, who we are, and all we can be. Blessings always speak of bounty and abundance. They remind us of what is and what might happen, even in a world that can turn on us more quickly than we could ever imagine. That day with Millicent and that night in the pub, in both the blessing I offered and the one I received, I glimpsed again the unique and sometimes untamed beauty of the church. It was brought back to me how much we have to offer because of how much we have received.

A worship service organizes our holiness like books on a shelf. It sets holiness straight out in front of us, then spells it out clearly for those of us slow to learn. Going to church gathers us together and lines us up and sits us down neatly for an hour and a bit once or twice a week so that we can be holy together. So much of what we are asked to do and to be happens best together; with those big splashes of encouragement we need to try to be holy. Church is a collaboration of holiness, a knitting together of loose threads and balls of yarn that makes everyone stronger and better and more beautiful.

This doesn't mean it's easy. It means it can be good.

My friend Deborah and I sat in Le Charlotte Café-Bistro in Mont Tremblant, Quebec, eating eggs Benedict and complaining, in church-lady fashion, about people who don't go to church. Between us, over five or six refills of coffee, we cobbled together a list of Bible study pals, neighbors, family members, seminary buddies, and old friends who have surprised us by dropping out of church. We were on a roll, tsking.

Then Deborah said, "I need church. Sometimes I need to just sit in the sanctuary. I need to hear Scripture read from up front. I need Communion." This isn't because Deborah's so strong—it's because she's so weak, like me. Just another church person on the way, bumbling along and occasionally having gleaming moments of clarity and calling. People do not attend church because they think they're so great; it's surely because they know they are not. They know they need God's mercy and the body to hold them in, to haul them back up on the life raft when they slip off, and to remind them, again and again, that they are holy and that they get to act that way. You are in this boat with us.

"Let us hold fast the confession of our hope without wavering, for he who promised is faithful," says the writer of Hebrews. "And let us consider how to stir up one another to love and good works, not neglecting to meet together, as is the habit of some, but encouraging one another, and all the more as you see the Day drawing near."[5] Church is a kind nurse and a stern doctor. She wraps us in bandages, sets our brokenness for healing, and then pushes us back out into the world to keep living in a way that, to do well, means we will have to stretch a bit. It's okay to be stretched.

9

REMEMBERING

ONE AFTERNOON, BRENT AND I collapsed onto our bed
for our ritualistic Friday afternoon nap. Van Morrison's "Into the
Mystic" streamed like a wide satin ribbon from the speaker we had
set up to mask the noises from the family who thump through
rooms and down the stairs like heavy hares on the other side of
our duplex walls. The music did more than cover up noise. It carried me in and over years and across miles and back to a rainy day
in Halifax when we sat on a wooden bench at the long and worn
tables of the Seahorse Tavern, probably on a Friday afternoon. We
had barely begun.

"Remember?" I said to Brent as we nap-cuddled in the sunlight
that came through the window. "Remember how young we were?
We'd sit there for hours." He smiled and dozed off.

We had changed so much. So had the Seahorse Tavern. It used to be dark all day long and packed full of sailors, students, and cigarette smoke. It was a gritty bar blocks up from the harbor in a port city that was also a university town. When we last visited the Seahorse on a trip back to Halifax, we couldn't find it right away. It had picked itself up, dusted itself off, and moved several blocks away to a better part of town. It stood proudly above ground and shone brightly with much higher-watt lightbulbs and person-sized windows.

The Seahorse looked better. We looked worse. But I do believe our insides were a little improved by then from all the practicing of our faith that we had been doing. Our hearts were wiser and more tender from all the love we had attempted. Our fears had shrunk. Our confidence had grown. I worried less about money. Brent worried less about me worrying about money and all the other things there are in this world to fret over. God's patience with us had made us patient with each other. God's forgiveness of us had helped us forgive each other the trespasses of a long marriage. We had seen God's tender faithfulness stretched out over the arc of our story, and contentment was beginning to be our companion. We had learned so much from people in the church about all that can go wrong and right in a life, and how a hurt life can still be a good life because of God. Some fruit had grown and now hung ripe on the tree.

It's often easier to notice the softening in our bodies and our abilities. But we soften also in our hearts, and in our souls and in our speech. Our dreams for our lives stretch and soften. After some time in the faith, we can love better because of what Jesus has done and what we have learned and seen and held and released. We love better because of all that has been lost and some of what has been found.

It is so good to be quiet in the sun with Jesus and Van Morrison and your true love. It is good to notice that it is good. Is it wrong to sometimes admire how the soul has grown wiser and softer and more expansive through seasons come and seasons gone of trying to walk with your arm looped through the arm of Jesus? It is good to notice and also to have another reason to say thank you. It's good to know that we have grown.

Acknowledging positive change in our lives from the long practice of holiness doesn't mean we are peacocks, strutting around the church hall and down the street. We know why we have been able to change and grow, and we are thankful. We can be confident of this, says Paul to you and me and the church in Philippi, that Jesus who began a good work in us will carry it "on to completion until the day of Christ Jesus."[1]

On this very day we are somewhere between the beginning and the completion. It began. It will be completed. We are drifting down a river of God's holiness, kicking with our feet and paddling along with our hands. We bob and spin, we make progress and then float around in the same spot for a while. We get nudged by a floating branch. Our feet hit bottom. The water is cold. Now it is warm. We are moving onward, toward the day of our completion, carried along by God's great affection.

The holy God draws us forward, closer and closer. We are moved and we are changed. God acts. We change. We act. We see how we need to change. We catch our breath. We lose it. God surrounds us. Our memories of those times and places and moments of God acting spectacularly, or very quietly and almost imperceptibly so that you can barely tell God is in the room, are all markers in our spiritual journeys that we can turn to when we need them. We will need them. We will need to remember when we saw God so closely or felt him like the gentlest of breezes, because there will be so many times when we feel like God is distant.

Back in the Old Testament, they would often build a memory prompt with work-worn hands to mark the places. In Joshua, twelve men picked up twelve large stones from the middle of the Jordan River, then piled them up in the Promised Land so they would remember that God had helped them cross the river with the Ark of the Covenant in a miraculous way. God told them to build the memorial. We can assume that God knew they would need help remembering, so he gave them those clear instructions on how to remember. In 1 Samuel, the prophet chose a stone and called it an *ebenezer*, which means "stone of help," as a memorial to how God had saved them in battle. We do need our ebenezers. We need to remember where we came from, and we need to remember our God, who every now and then was so obvious that our faith was fueled for the next mile and a half.

Most of us do not build a memorial with a pile of rocks and our bare hands when God acts in a way that gives us a direct and undeniable brush with his holiness. Our memorials are in our minds, or our journals, and in the stories of encouragement we share with each other about God showing up holy in our lives, and making our lives holy.

The low ground of faith is more common for a lot of us than the high mountain peaks. Often, there is more grind than glory. A dogged kind of commitment might be required for some of us, and a stick-to-itiveness that can feel like work. This is especially true for those of us who prefer a little hard proof every now and then. It's no accident that John starts his first letter with this reassurance of the tangibility of God: "That which was from the beginning, which we have heard, which we have seen with our eyes, which we have looked at and our hands have touched—this we proclaim concerning the Word of life."[2] The reminder of the seen-ness and heard-ness of Jesus among us is bread and water and walking shoes for the journey, if we let it be. It is soul sustenance. We have our very own seen and heard moments of Jesus in our lives, even if they are quiet. Take note. We should write them down. We can forget even the moments that we could not fathom ever forgetting. Not many people stay for long on the mountaintop.

The Christian liturgical year itself is built in the valleys and on the mountains. Christmas and Easter are the two biggies, of course, when God plants a flag in hearts and history. Jesus comes in like a lamb and goes out like a lion. The world is forever changed, and so are we. The church seasons—these high feasts—throb with theology and meaning and symbol and beauty and truth (and songs and special prayers, depending on your tradition, and food), but for most of us they only come around twice a year.

Much of the space between one high and magnificent season and the other is called Ordinary Time. Better Anglicans than me, and certainly better ministers' wives, can tell you about the colors and the sashes and the frontals that drape the altars to remind us what season we are currently in. The ordinary is a low road and a steady path, a series of days and weeks and months that turn into years that are lived out steadily and usually without hoopla, and then there you are once again ascending a mountain or slipping down the slope you didn't expect and never would have wanted, right into a valley.

In the ordinary times and in the valleys, we do better and stay stronger if we can remember God and our closer times with the Holy One. Remembering is a spiritual act. Holy memories help us. Turning our attention deliberately back to remember a time of certainty and intimacy with God—a time when we could feel and almost taste the holiness surrounding us—helps sustain us when the pickings are slim. Remembering helps us trust in God and live and love out of our identity as holy people set aside by God to lead holy lives to God's glory. Remembering is an act of faithfulness.

When we are on the mountaintop, our job is to just be present and try to appreciate the view and take notes, if we can. We will need them for later, when the remembering is required. We will need what we gather up there in the good and close times, during the quiet miracles of closeness to God, and when we know that Jesus is with us. We need the words, the sounds, the smells—that which we have heard and seen and the very almost touch of King Jesus—for the rest of the long time when we will need the memories of the mountain moments to carry us. This is not sad, necessarily. It's just true, and it's because we are simply people, after all. We need to ask for and listen to the holy stories of others also, for our edification, and probably theirs as well. There is power in both telling and hearing.

Being part of the body as we are, we aren't just left with our own memories to sift through. We have a collective memory as God's people. We share a holy and epic yesterday. God showing up and parting the Red Sea for the escaping Israelites becomes our memory as well when we are grafted onto the vine and adopted into this family. Jesus whispering "Mary" to his grieving friend outside the empty tomb on Easter morning is part of our story now too. We pull it forth when we need a blanket, a pillow, or a drink of cold water. When we need Jesus to look on us fully and say our name out loud, we can remember that Jesus said "Mary."

The Bible is full of *Remember this and that*, and *Don't forget these things that you have seen and heard and touched and tasted, because you will need to remember*. Scripture is the memoir of God. "Let each generation tell its children of your mighty acts; let them proclaim your power," says Psalm 145:4. We need our stories. This is part of what church is about. We hear the stories of our faith ancestors and how they wandered and when they waited. We hear they also wondered, just like us. We need to be reminded of when and where God showed up to put them out of the misery of not understanding, or to lead them into battle. Our memory becomes our comfort, our solace, and our companion when we feel alone. God's story is a big story of which we now are a small part.

What are our stories of redemption? What are our holy memories? Those are good questions to ask ourselves every now and then. There will come a time when we need them to carry us forward in our faith. There will be times when all the air will leave the room. The fire may die and the pillar of cloud evaporate. We might get lost. Things can just be so ordinary for so long that a deep discouragement settles in. We will feel alone if we rely on our feelings alone and not our solid and practical memory and all we know about the God who loves us.

That is what a holy memory is for and why God reminds us again and again to remember, and maybe even build a little ebenezer there in that spot to help us do that. Yes, right there.

A friend asked me once to accompany her to a charismatic church service, a gathering unlike anything I had ever attended.

"I want to be slain in the Spirit," she said. "And I don't want to go alone." She confided to me her history of attending worship events like this one with other friends who always seemed to have supernatural brushes with God, but those encounters never happened for her. My friend was always the bridesmaid and never the bride, charismatically speaking. She told me how this pattern had strained some relationships. She believed that some of her friends felt spiritually superior to her after watching her left high and dry at the altar.

"I'm sure that's not the case. I can't imagine they would feel that way," I said.

And then I said: "I'll go with you. I'm your girl."

We drove out to the airport one Sunday night, where the congregation known for its visible manifestations of the Holy Spirit met in a cavernous room like a warehouse. There was a worship time more enthusiastic than I was accustomed to, a vigorous sermon, and then the invitation to line up to be prayed over by church leaders.

"Do you want me to come up front with you?" I asked her, uncertain of the extent of my supportive role. She said yes.

So up we went. A stranger put their hands on me, and down I sank, right to the floor, where I lay in the warmth of God's love. I lay slain until I began to worry that the zipper of my pants was down, and the spell of love was broken. Clearly, it was time to stand up again. I had been floating in a tiny little ocean of tranquility, until I worried. These feelings I had of warm accord and deep awareness of how real God was and how deep was God's love for me, how personal and precise God's regard, lasted for approximately two weeks. It was a hangover of holiness that helped me stay in the best mood I had been in for years. My children's shenanigans did not ruffle me. I slept better. I thoroughly enjoyed myself for fourteen days. Also, and I believe this began on the drive home from the service, a spiritual smugness crept into my feelings about my friend and her lack of slainness.

She was right, I realized, amazed. I had joined her other bad friends in thinking there must have been something deserving of me to receive such a gift. This part of the story, which I remember all too well, is another example of why I don't see how holier-than-thou can really be a thing in the lives of honest saints. Always we keep company with ourselves. We have changed, but not yet fully. We see, but not yet clearly. We love, but not yet really.

Since that night, years have passed. That kind of physical brush with the Holy Spirit has only happened to me that once, and to be fair, I have only once put myself in the Spirit's way in that manner. I prefer the stand, the sit, and the kneel at church, rather than the optional laying-down bits, or the dancing. Still, it is good for me to remember both the lovey-dovey feeling that wrapped around me for days and the spiritual stuntedness that I saw in myself—and repented of as much as I could—toward my friend, to whom I never actually confessed. I was too ashamed. The years, or maybe just that night, drifted us apart, and that happens too among the saints. That is what I remember, and the remembering helps me understand, and maybe be better the next time.

⌒

Remembering is not going backward, but actually a way we can move forward. Our memories of encounters with God's holiness can sustain us for our own journey deeper in and further out, into our own holy callings in the world. In the Bible, when God tells his people to remember how he rescued them with harrowing escapes from danger, or how he provided through fire and water and manna, it seems God is trying to fortify them in that moment, and also to prepare them for what's to come next. It's a hug and a nudge. Maybe, back then, it became a little stressful to even hear the word *remember*. *Remember that time when we all escaped from slavery and God showed up again and again . . .* Well, guess what? Something is about to happen that will require much of us, and even though we might be frightened or just very tired, we can move ahead, assured that God will show up again. Or maybe it's just that we are entering into a long patch where things will go quiet and be hard, and we will be asked to stay the course, and to not be so panicky or full of bellyaching.

Remember this, so you don't worry about that. I have already taught you things. You know some stuff. You're not a baby anymore. Something is coming, and soon. Or we might be remembering so we can wait better, and with more patience for God to act. Waiting is hard.

Remembering when God acted in the past can help us believe that our waiting is a holy act in itself because of God's holiness and faithfulness to us. God can take God's own sweet time. Remembering is not a passive act. Our memories of holiness reach back to stretch us forward. To remember is to stretch and bend and reach and sometimes leap. Remembering seems to lead somewhere new, and maybe better. As a spiritual discipline, remembering is about the present and the future. There is more to come, and we will be stronger for it because of what has already happened. To be as brave as we will need to be, we reach back to what has already come to pass. We will all need to be very brave.

I have a notebook on my bedside table where I mark down what's bugging me and what's bringing me joy. This is Cindy Bunch's idea, from her book *Be Kind to Yourself.* She suggests it as a pared-down daily examen, that longer Ignatian practice of con-templating where God showed up in a day or when we felt God's absence. Where did we respond faithfully, and where did we not? I do this practice most nights now, off and on, as sporadically as most other disciplines that I know can make me strong. I'm on year three of my "Read the Bible in One Year" program. I slog, not sprint. It is okay. It will be okay.

At the beginning of this practice, I usually listed only one item under what bugged me and one under what brought me joy. It took work to think of more than one thing. I had to train my mind to cast back and remember. Then, one day under *joy*, I wrote about walking and listening to a podcast and baking cookies for my neighbor. I felt a ping of release. From that day on, my lists grew. I remembered more. At first, mostly the bad-things list grew, and then, more slowly, the joy list. That's usually how these things go. I could feel Brent's nervousness beside me as I scribbled my list in bed. He knew that sometimes he simply *had* to be appearing on the wrong side of the page, and of course that was true. Because we are who we are, it is normal for most of us to remember first and fully the bad things. The bad stands tall in our memories, towering over everything else, even in just a single day. We let our disappointments take us lower than the pleasant surprises take us higher. Desolation can outweigh consolation.

This can be true on a daily basis, but also in an epic, lifelong kind of way. What went so wrong is there at our fingertips. To see what is missing is so easy and obvious. The excruciating is undeniable, much more so than what went right, what was there, and what was wonderful. We can forget the good so easily. That is why faithful remembering is a discipline. We are predisposed to cling to our disappointments, and maybe especially our shame.

What does this have to do with the holiness of God and the holy lives God calls us into? God remembers us and forgets our sin. But we remember our sin and forget God, or we crouch in our shame instead of standing in our forgiveness. This is how our holy remembering can change us, help us feel like and live like the holy people God wants us to remember we already are. When we believe and accept who God says we are—a holy people, cleansed from our iniquities, with our sin set away from us as far as the east is from the west[3]—then we can believe that we are called and made capable to lead a holy life. We can believe that we are leading a holy life right now, already, because we remember that God remembered us, but forgot our sin.

Psalm 103 is like an overpacked suitcase of how God loves us in this way: "Let all that I am praise the LORD; may I never forget the good things he does for me. He forgives all my sins and heals all my diseases. He redeems me from death and crowns me with love and tender mercies. He fills my life with good things. My youth is renewed like the eagle's!"[4]

Each line is a holy reminder of who God is and what God does—and therefore, who we are and who we can be. We can do the work God has called us to do because of the work that God is doing already inside us and in the world.

Later, when I shared with a spiritual director about my daily lists of bothering and happiness, she asked me what I did with the lists. "Nothing," I answered, caught once again in laziness. She suggested I take things a step further and thank God for the good and pray about the bad.

"I will do that," I said. "That's a good idea." I like it when spiritual directors tell us exactly what to do. I began that night. I prayed with my BIC marker in my hand and with the help of little doodles, another tip from Cindy's book. I drew a little heart beside every good thing that day and said, "Thank you." Beside my small and big disappointments, I drew a cross to remind Jesus, and I said, "Please."

⌒

Church helps us with the spiritual habit of cultivating a holy memory, or a memory predisposed to remember the holy. This is part of what church does for us—the gathering, the waving and nodding to each other, and the sermon. Weekly we remember, because weekly we need to and are guided along in that work of remembering, which also feels like love. In our worship, we receive and remember who God is and who we are now and who we are meant to be. Sometimes, when our kids would be going off somewhere to do heaven-knows-what with goodness-knows-who, I would say, "Remember who you are!" as they walked out the door. I did this to ruin their fun. I hoped they would do some things and not do other things because they were tucked into Christ. I wanted them to live out of the dignity of their belonging, to inch high and not tumble low.

In our particular church tradition, we confess out loud every Sunday. We acknowledge that "we have left undone those things which we ought to have done, and we have done those things we ought not to have done; and apart from your grace, there is no health in us."[5] Before we say these lines out loud, we hold silence briefly. In the quiet there is an invitation to do the private work of remembering the week that has just flowed through our fingertips like water, and to bring to mind the near misses and the falls. We can remember the mistakes we made and the injuries we inflicted and sustained. It is a micro-examen of our week. Mind drift is normal, and if you start to make plans for later, you can be forgiven for that, too.

We always read a psalm responsively by the whole verse. Then someone throws a hammer in and we're told to read responsively by the half verse, and always someone gets it wrong, sometimes the priest. Where one person is supposed to be speaking alone, others join in. Where others are to join in, someone is speaking alone. There is nervous laughter. People turn to see who laughed. We find our place again, and proper rhythm is restored.

"I remember the days of old. I ponder all your great works and think about what you have done," reads the person assigned to Psalm 143:5. It might be Marilyn called to this mission, this holy task of standing in front of the church and reading well and carefully. Her eyes are on us, her co-participants in remembering out loud together, because she clearly practiced. Reading the psalms out loud together is important and ancient. It is a call to remember, and a plea to be sustained.

"I lift my hands to you in prayer. I thirst for you as parched land thirsts for rain,"[6] we answer Marilyn back. Those are our assigned lines and our assigned lot. Here is an acknowledgement of our pondering and our plight. We are standing in someone else's words, someone specific who had a height and a history, a favorite color and food; someone who slept on the right side or preferred the left, who spoke for themselves but also a community, and for us who were yet to come. I wonder if they knew that they wrote what was true for then, but also for now and always?

In just one week, we can live out an entire psalm. Each day is a verse. We can start drifting very soon after walking out those big front doors on Sunday, checking the time and finding ourselves on the sidewalk, debating where to go for lunch. By Monday, we are lost. By Tuesday, frustration. Wednesday can bowl us over with its disappointments. Thursday, we are on our knees, if we can manage that. Friday, we plead for mercy. Saturday is nothingness, plus Costco, and by Sunday, we can barely show up, but hopefully we do. We shift ourselves into worship again. We are ready to be reminded of all that is good and true and ancient. That's how you live an honest psalm in the space of a week.

And what is a sermon but a long, well-thought-out reminder? When Christmas and Easter roll around—those annual seasons when I have so often seen Brent carving out time to write another new sermon that he sweated over—I have wondered, *How hard can it be?*

Sometimes I even said it out loud. "Does it have to be this difficult every time? Haven't you preached this a million times?"

"It's always different," he would say.

It is old, but it is also always new. It's all been heard before and now again, as if for the first time. Nothing has changed and everything has, including our own wobbly selves who need to be brought back in again, called, and corralled. It is the preacher's job to remind us, and themselves, every week, and we'd like them to do it especially well and artfully on those high feast days when we have brought our nephews and our neighbors. Preachers know this, and they feel that pressure. Many of them feel nauseated Saturday evening and nap most of Sunday afternoon.

What they are doing is proclaiming the mystery of faith again and again, which in our tradition we repeat also every week as people sitting in the pew, and this is it: Christ has died. Christ is risen. Christ will come again.

We enact that also in Communion. "This is my body, broken for you. When you do this, remember me." Communion is the very way that Jesus told us to remember. Remembering is baked into holiness since the beginning. With the Eucharist we remember physically by walking up to receive the bread and the wine, which we will chew and swallow in these bodies that are set aside for God. We stand and kneel, maybe. We watch others move up for Communion in that line that holds so much sorrow and so much joy in the hearts of those who stand in it with us. We see that we are not alone, that we are part of this body. And that helps us be the holy people God has told us we are and asked us to be.

Our rescue takes place individually and together, and we can usually remember it best as a group, as a church. We remember together in that line, hands open wide in front of us to receive. We are made strong for what is to come. What is to come, both the joy and the sorrow, we cannot even imagine.

10

SORROW

SORROW CAME TO US on a cold November afternoon. There I
sat, oblivious, three provinces away, sipping tea and chatting about
the neighbors at my parents' kitchen table. Back home, Brent sat
at our dining room table on a Zoom meeting, struggling to hold
up his end of a conversation with Glenn, one of his lay leaders.
Brent seemed confused, and they decided to finish the meeting
later. He lay down on the couch for a nap. Uneasy, Glenn called
Elise and David, a young couple who were also leaders in the
church and lived close to us. He suggested they go pound on our
door and make sure Brent was okay. My groggy and surprised
husband eventually answered, invited them in, and talked about
Disneyland. They went to the emergency room, just in case.

This is not a book about all the sadness that can befall us or the sorrows that can eclipse everything that is beautiful in the world. It is meant to be about trying to touch holiness around us and nurture holiness within us. It is about seeing and witnessing and living into holiness here and now. But now I know that sorrow will come, no matter what we do or who we are trying to slowly become. There is almost no end to what is possible within the wild brokenness of our lives unfolding in this world. We all suspect this, but we cannot guess. The knowledge of all that can go wrong crouches at the edge of our consciousness and shows up in the dreams we have that leave us unsettled the next morning. "I had such a bad sleep last night," we say to someone who loves us, and we check to see that the sun is still in the sky and everyone is accounted for.

Soon after Brent's kidney transplant, his health had seemed restored. He flushed pink again and had an energy he hadn't felt for years. "It's Brent 2.0!" said Pastor Michelle, a priest on his team. She was right. The transplant was a reset. Brent took his electric guitar out of its case and bought new pedals to add to his collection. He moved through the house in a cloud of music from the phone he carried with him everywhere, for that very purpose. He shaved to Van Morrison and ate blueberries and vanilla yogurt to Bach. He had his life back, and he filled it with music.

Most days, Brent walked to the church wearing a bright-orange backpack that had been abandoned in the empty nest by one of our kids. He zigzagged his way through the core of the city in a manner I critiqued as inefficient. Up Flora, across Kent, turn onto Gladstone but not for long, up Bay, down Gilmour, and by this slower path he wound his way to the church. He paused to take photos he posted on Facebook in an album named Centretown. Purple delphiniums spilled out from an inner-city front garden, and he captioned them *Joy overfloweth on Flora St.* Our kids were amused. Their single-minded father, who was reluctant to climb into a canoe without a thoroughly discussed plan and clearly stated goal, was meandering his way to work photographing ivy-covered houses and "One day at a time" messages written in loopy letters with sidewalk chalk on a driveway. "I'm going to make this kidney last," Brent said.

We shopped in outdoor stores for wide-brimmed hats that were not too ridiculous, for the sake of variety. Brent coated himself with sunscreen every morning in front of the mirror in our little bathroom off the kitchen, John Coltrane or Wynton Marsalis the soundtrack to his caution. He counted out a fistful of pills and fired each bottle back into his medicine bag with a thunk. I observed, sipping the Americano he made me from his beloved espresso machine in our kitchen's Corner of Conflict, so called because there we were always in each other's way. He had begun to make me breakfast most mornings and brought it to me as I read the paper, which should have been no big deal, but for me, it was tender.

In a transplant recipient, drugs are used to suppress the immune system that keeps us untransplanted people safe, and this is so their body does not reject their new organ. But the body pays a steep price. Skin cancer is one of the possible side effects of immune suppression. We were very mindful of skin cancer. Brent worried he wouldn't be able to relax ever again in a warm, turquoise ocean under the sun that was no longer friend. A longer life was worth it, of course, but we saw that we had hiked with determination out of one forest only to find ourselves stumbling through another.

Most of the things that can go very wrong are rare. They had not preoccupied us.

At the hospital that night in November, they ordered a CT scan. Our daughter had replaced Elise and David by then and was with

Brent in the little curtained cubicle when the doctors rushed back in holding a waiver for a biopsy. Brent had seven dark shadows on his brain.

~

A few weeks before Brent was hospitalized, we had taken the train to Quebec City for a short vacation. Brent recorded the flat countryside flashing by and posted it on Facebook with lines from the hymn "Rock of Ages" as the caption. *Rock of ages cleft for me, let me hide myself in thee*, he typed. I don't know why he chose those particular words for that image on that morning, but it does bring me comfort now.

Brent was never afraid to share his faith on Facebook or anywhere else. Pastors rarely are, of course. We would find such hesitation strange. We expect pastors to be the leaders in the telling of faith and in all things holy. We count on them to be the ones who will always share the truth of Jesus Christ and God's love, and not be squeamish like the rest of us babies.

Brent was just an ordinary guy trying to live a holy life by God's grace. That's what he would say, if someone were to ask. He had been called, and despite all his fear and misgivings, he had answered.

Brent had gentled over the years. He listened more and welcomed in before he witnessed. He was comfortable on the edges with the doubters and the questioners, all the dwellers on the outskirts. Also, Brent loved the funny ducks. He knew that they sometimes could be the prophets.

His sermons were bolder. I'd wander off to the washroom because sometimes I was an awful minister's wife, too easily embarrassed by vigor or volume. If someone complimented him on a sermon while I milled around waiting for him after church, I'd hear him say, "Praise God!" This was a new response for him. "Why don't you just say thank you?" I asked. Now I wonder when I became so grouchy.

Brent loved that train and our trip. A train in November sways beside empty swing sets and rusty cars, fields that lie fallow and, thankfully, the evergreens. We held hands. We made plans. Our Airbnb was a one-room bachelor flat in a century home down a cobblestoned alleyway in Quebec City. We admired wide-plank floors and a rock wall built from stones that were pulled from the earth before we were born and will last long after we are both gone. We went on a walking tour through the cold with a guide who pointed out basilicas, recounted battles, and told the story of the massive stone wall built to keep the enemies out. We saw Engelbert Humperdinck in concert, a birthday gift to me that had been strange enough to make me feel deeply seen and so loved by my husband.

Brent loved Quebec City. "I could live here," he said. "We need to come back in the summer." Then, as we continued down the narrow street, I realized my husband wasn't beside me. He crouched on his hands and feet on the street, just fallen. "I got really dizzy," he said. We walked through the snow that fell heavily on the fortified city and found a pub serving French onion soup. It was a full blizzard by then, and there were only a few other patrons. We sat by the window, where I couldn't stop my crying. Brent explained to the waitress that he had fallen, and that I was a worrywart.

When I look at the photos from our trip, I can see so clearly now what we could not see then. Eyes as blue as a sky look out from a pale, tired face.

⌒

What do you do when you do not know what to do? You stand guard around that painful bed. Your children rise up beside you.

Call Nana and Papa. Do it gently.
What do we tell the church?
He looks good today!
Someone said it could just be an infection.
Did you hear him laugh? Did you see him smile?
Let him try to feed himself.
This morning he said his name.

We prayed. The first of two hospitals where Brent stayed, the one where he declined the little sandwich bag of family photos I brought because "photos mean a long stay," was a twenty-minute walk from our house. Walking was easier for me than parking. One morning, as I marched up the hill to the hospital on Carling Avenue, I matched my praying to the rising and falling of my boots on the snowy sidewalk. "Please, Jesus," right foot up. "Save him," left foot down.

And as clear as a bell you do not want to hear, I felt God's reply in the deep place: "Stop pleading. Start welcoming me in." I feared then that we were in the valley that is known for all the things you do not want to ever happen.

Daily, things got worse. A heartbreaking huddle of doctors shared the diagnosis of post-transplant lymphoproliferative disorder with my daughter and me, as we sat on a couch in a hospital corridor. The shadows were lesions. The lesions were cancer. The kind nurse with the pink hair who occasionally patted my shoulder unhooked him from antibiotics to fight the infection we had hoped he had, and bundled him onto a stretcher headed for the other hospital for the chemotherapy that would not work.

In the valley of the shadow of death, I feared evil. I tried to believe that the Shepherd was with us because to not believe would be worse. I knew that. But the rod and the staff, they did not comfort me.

People comforted us, and I saw that this was probably how it worked. As I write, I am only newly arrived on this planet of grief and early into being transported against my will into a storyline I never expected. I have only just begun to learn. I do know that. But I came to understand early on that God's comfort can arrive most obviously, for me at least, in the shape of other people. The church, family, friends, neighbors, the guy who shovels our driveway—they all emerged from the valley sides carrying tiny bits of light. The Shepherd was present, I thought I saw, in the noble bakers, the knitters of prayer shawls, the people who cleaned our house, the lasagna and chili makers. In the valley of the shadow of death, there is so much lasagna. Trays are left on doorsteps or transferred steaming hot, encased in foil wrap, from one set of hands to the other. *Thank you*. Those who could eat ate. The food reminded us we weren't completely alone in this changed world. Jesus is a good cook. Here was the small evidence of things not seen.

This valley would be long and hard, the path through chaotic. The one person who could have guided us lay in the bed before us. Brent had told us all along that we could do holy and hard things through God's grace and our own surprising grit. I saw this was so. I wondered if we had strength because of the prayers of hundreds who knew by then that Brent was in deep trouble.

One day, lying in his bed beside him, I whispered the order of our lives into his ear, through the story of the places we'd lived from one side of the country to the other. First, there was Halifax,

I said. Remember? The top floor of an old brick apartment with all those stairs to climb? We watched the Persian Gulf War on the television in the Holiday Inn lounge on the corner of Quinpool and Robie. And then Vancouver in that pricey basement apartment with the thick carpet. I was the tour guide of our life together and he the patient witness. I described each place as well as I could remember it on that day, and I saw how the years had been full and beautiful and were now flowing through our hands like water, and away from us.

My friend Tracy came to the hospital and sat with me at the coffee shop in the lobby where the baristas still found the nerve to tell their customers to have a good day. She held my hands as I swayed unmoored across from her, and she reminded me about Jesus, Mary, Martha, and their brother Lazarus, and how Jesus had cried at suffering and death. There were no answers to the why, just the reminder of Jesus who cried with his friends who grieved. That moment was my movement over to Jesus who hung on the cross, and a reminder to me of that first forsakenness. Because sometimes, we did feel so forsaken. That lonely Shepherd made sense to me, more than any talk of victory or miracles or promises.

For years Brent had invited me to help serve Communion at church. For years I had declined. I was afraid of the church people who take things into their own hands, literally. What if I thought they had the cup and they thought I had the cup and we dropped that cup? Red wine spilled on the floor and horrified glances turned my way terrified me. I had never held the cup to anyone's mouth or placed a wafer on a tongue until Brent's fishing buddy, Doug, drove for hours from up north in week two to serve Brent Communion.

During his six weeks of dying, my husband moved in and out of dark caves. The day Doug came to the sixth-floor cancer ward,

Brent was sunk into himself and very far away from us. I took the goblet from Doug's outstretched hand and lifted it to my husband's mouth. I held it for him, tightly, and he drank the whole thing down. I placed the wafer in his mouth. "Chew it," I said. "Now swallow."

We had more pastors available to us than you could shake a stick at, plus a bishop. There was Brent's own team from the church, but also just friends in the ministry who lived far and near. Clergy befriend clergy, or they do if they know what is good for them.

When we began to see things clearly, we called Steven, a pastor from another Anglican church in the city. "Will you be his priest?" I asked.

Steven agreed, and over the steep mountain climb of Brent's illness, he did the work of a friend-priest. He visited. He sat. He listened and spoke. He worked to understand what Brent was trying to say, and sometimes he had to guess like the rest of us. He prayed and anointed his friend with oil. Then, when the days were short and the hallway was crowded with parents, his brother, my sister, crying cousins, and only the dearest and rarest of friends, we called Steven. "Come soon."

Steven passed out pamphlets called "Ministry at the Time of Death" to my children and me so we could join in as one priest prayed God's mercy onto and into the other. Sometimes we believe that it will not be possible for us to even breathe through the hardest of things, let alone say a refrain. My husband's last rites were like that for me. I thought we would all once again fall to our knees. But the certainty in Steven's voice that the God of mercy would absolutely receive Brent into his heavenly Kingdom kept us upright. We knew that, yes, it would certainly please God to grant my husband, these beautiful children's good father, my church's pastor "a place of refreshment and everlasting blessedness," and that Brent would be imminently receiving joy and gladness with the other saints in light. We were assured and so we had assurance. It was a blessed assurance, and it was holy, and we each knew it. To know what is true when the ground is crumbling beneath you can be understood as a blessing, when you are scrambling for anything at all that looks like blessing.

At the end of my husband's calling, we heard from hundreds of people from the churches Brent had served about what an impact he had on their lives. No one mentioned an excellent sermon he had preached. We heard about the quiet attendance of Brent in their lives. He paid attention. He made space. Brent was a good companion to people searching for holiness. "Just as you are, let's pray," he would start worship services. He acknowledged out loud the rough weeks people might have had, full of doing things they ought not to have done, and not doing things they ought to have done, as the confession says. He lived his weeks like that too. He ended Sunday services reminding people they were now free to leave, live, and love just a little bit different, just a tiny bit better, and that we could all do it. It was also a reminder to himself.

Brent ran a tight ship of a funeral. He trusted the liturgy that first makes room for an ocean of grief and then points to the nearby shore of hope. "I am the resurrection and the life, says the Lord. Whoever believes in me, though he die, yet shall he live, and everyone who lives and believes in me shall never die," Brent would read from John 11, the opening sentences of every funeral he ever led.[1] Once, he conducted a full funeral that not a single person attended. It was just Brent and a dead guy in the pastel parlor of a Toronto funeral home. "You did the whole thing with no one there?" I asked. "My job is the same whether anyone shows up or not," he said. But it did break his heart, that someone would be so alone in their death and in their farewell.

Brent did not die alone. He died in the middle of a January morning in a room wallpapered with dozens of photos and strung with white twinkly lights. He died in a bed with a wife, a daughter, two sons, and a daughter-in-law piled on and around, holding him, kissing him, weeping over him, holding his body and his gaze and saying thank you over and over again to and for this man to whom God had given such grace to lead a holy life.

11

HOLINESS

HERE AND NOW

"GIVE US GRACE, GOD, to lead a holy life." Pastor Michelle stood in front of a small group of worshipers scattered throughout the sanctuary, raised her hands in supplication, and prayed on behalf of us all.

What is a holy life here and now? I wondered, for me and for my fellow worshipers, all of us in states of disrepair: from severely crushed or mangled, as I heard in one recent sermon, to mildly broken, to nearing wholeness. Thanks be to God for glimpses of our wholeness. I glanced around. Because it was a time of prayer—and not a time for glancing around—I witnessed friends kneeling on old-padded benches, eyes closed, hands clasped, the heavy weight of their worlds so obvious. Others stood, coats still on in the dampness of an old sanctuary where it was not quite spring yet. One woman glanced at her watch. The church bat swooped low, as it sometimes does, causing its customary ripples of consternation. From such different lives we had all arrived at this common place and common core calling to live our painful, joyful, wildly unpredictable, safe, and so dangerous lives as holy. The invitation to holiness—so uncomfortable and so promising both—was freely given from God to us.

Paul wrote to Timothy and reminded us that "he has saved us and called us to a holy life—not because of anything we have done but because of his own purpose and grace."[1] Here is the promise we can try to believe and try to live out with curiosity and intention. The opportunities to live out of the acceptance of our own holiness given by God are everywhere, all around us, all the time. Being holy is rolled-up sleeves and hands dirty from digging in the garden, and also it is sitting in the sun. It is work and it is rest. Holy living can happen by accident, but it also happens deeply on purpose. Being holy is not just who we are, but it is also what we choose to do. It is the presence of God on the inside and the practice of Jesus on the outside. We have been set apart so we can fully engage. Our holiness will look ragged and rough and incomplete. We will have a clumsy practice of it. We can ask God to help us and give us the grace we need. We are safe to try to lead a holy life.

One morning, at a women's breakfast at church, I admired a fellow attendee's necklace, strung from wooden beads with tiny carved elephants. It looked like it had been carefully chosen at a market stall full of carvings and batiks, as a remembrance of a trip abroad.

"I love it," I told her, partly to make conversation, as we do.

"Thank you," she said. She lifted one of the little elephants in her hand and began to say something more about it, or so I assumed. I prepared myself to hear the origin story of the necklace.

"I can't think of the word," she said instead, tapping its tiny carved head with one finger.

"Would you like me to help you?" I offered. I said this because I knew my aging friend sometimes struggled to find words. I also knew, from experience, that she didn't always like it when people finished her sentences for her, as we do.

"No, thank you," she said. "I'd rather come up with it myself." Small elephant in hand, my friend searched for her lost word. I was tempted to change the subject, but I was trying to respect her wishes and it was early on a Saturday, and I didn't have much else to talk about. So I waited.

It felt like an hour passed, but it had to have only been a few moments. "It's time to eat!" someone called out, and the pair of us, not having uttered another word, shared a smile and moved toward the buffet line.

I was the speaker at this breakfast, so I was eager to fill my plate quickly. I hurried over to the long table pushed up against a wall, laden with food because women cook very well for each other, and secured the second place in line.

First in line was one of the ladies in our church who often depends on a walker to get around, which also serves as a portable table for her books and bags when she's having a chat, and a perch for when she needs a little rest.

She inched her walker down the length of the buffet, as anyone with a walker would.

Watching and waiting, I boldly discerned that my older sister must need my help to manage her walker and the plate she filled from the array of quiches, warm muffins, plump blueberries, and, wonderfully, morning brownies. I stepped out from behind her, took the plate right out of her hand, and forced myself upon her buffet experience. "Let me help you," I said, and just before she answered, I imagined the other women observing the servant's heart of their priest's wife. I felt warm.

"No, thank you," she said, and took her plate right back from me. I stepped back and into my proper place behind her, no longer trying to rush her or change things for my own comfort. We continued to creep down the buffet line, taking our own sweet time. As it turned out, no one needed or wanted my self-serving help. Frequently, that can happen.

A few months after this breakfast, I will look down the endless hallway of a funeral home on the afternoon of Brent's visitation. This saint will be sitting patiently at the end of it, walker in front of her, first in line once again. Pastor Michelle will go to her and say that she is a whole hour early and that she needs to stay put. This will make me feel loved by both of them, in slightly different ways.

Just after the breakfast, though, I stood at the back of the sanctuary during Communion and watched people come and go, as I like to do. Communion is the great equalizer. Here we all are together, however and whatever. We have sung songs and hymns, some of us poorly and others of us carrying the tune and tempo for the rest, and maybe really belting it out. There was singing. We have heard a sermon. We have tried to listen. My eyes would have met Brent's at some point, over some shared amusement over something that did not go as planned or was amusing and tender. There has been prayer. Minds have wandered. We have herded our thoughts back into rightful, better places, and maybe more than once. We have risen to our feet and sunk to our knees, as we are able, and if we want.

We have already prayed the Prayer of Humble Access that I

had found so difficult for its bold, bald reminder that we are not worthy and yet, because God's very character is always to have mercy, we can and we should and we may and we will be part of this holy life with its movements and motions.

The Sunday school kids have gone from and now returned to the service, like puppies. There has been chasing, consolation, and family reunions.

After they receive the bread-body and the wine-blood of Christ, people return to their seats via the middle aisle. It doesn't matter what part of the church you were sitting in, we all end up in that center aisle, unless we dart off to the washroom or to get the coffee going.

I observed the woman with the walker kneeling in prayer. As frail as she might seem, she could kneel in front of God much longer than most of us could hold such a posture of prayer. Her back was straight, her hands clasped in front of her, eyes closed, and her hair looked salon-visited for Sunday morning. My friend wore a fancy sweater with a lovely brooch. That's what a lot of senior lady saints do. Sometimes, holiness can have a pleasing Sunday morning look.

There also was my friend of the lost words, making her way slowly up the aisle and back to her seat. Behind her were parishioners who had slowed their pace to match hers, and to not overtake her. She was not rushed. She looked very peaceful, as we all usually feel after Communion. It's like we have tasted peace. She was oblivious to the small crowd swelled up behind her. The congregation moved gently behind her in what felt like a holy accompaniment. There is so much love to be given and accepted, offered and received, and so much love for someone paying attention to notice. We can better live a holy life together in a place that is devoted to that practice, at church.

Living a holy life does not need to be complicated. It can be simple. On some days, holiness can be about setting aside our desire to be the holy hero. It can be simply listening and not even speaking, especially if our speaking is all about telling someone else what's what. It is not holy to tell other people they are not holy. Can our posture of holiness toward each other be more loving than lecturing? God does not coerce. So we are free to not coerce, and instead to love. For most of us, this will come as a relief. We are strong enough to sit in humility's seat. We really are.

Holiness can be the smallest acts of love that we see in front of us, to which we say yes, even when it's ridiculously awkward. Our small acts of love, that gentle and maybe obvious work that is at our feet and hands when we open our eyes and look for it, are all part of helping the Kingdom come to its slow and inevitable arrival. We help build the Kingdom hourly, daily, and a little bit blindly. No one could ever deny the frailty of our efforts.

Living out of our holiness can mean not rushing people, or not finishing their sentences for them when their sentences matter so much. The small things do not mean that sometimes the request of holiness will not be gargantuan and marked by a depth of sacrifice that can double us over. We will gasp with it. We can live into and out of holiness even then if we step slowly through this forest, down this path, up this mountain. Through that valley. Others have done it; knowing that, we know it is possible. It might not be too much for us, after all. The saints before us and around us can help us see what is possible.

One thing I know for certain after my long attendance at church and being married to the minister is that we are prone to believe that everyone else is better at the Christian life than we are. This has been my abiding impression, that everyone thinks everyone else is holier than they are, and better suited. We have holiness envy. We think it's easy for other people. We think we are the absolute worst. Here, we find breathing room. It is a good place to start the journey. It is a much bigger problem if we think we are the best. Humility is the dark, rich soil from which holiness can stretch and bloom like a sunflower, face turned toward the sun. There is so much hope for all of us who think we are just too broken to be mended. We are mendable. We are holy. We can be the broken brave, and the brave broken, together.

What would it be like to talk honestly about holiness together? To reach up and bring the dusty word off the top shelf reserved for precious things and toss it around? Can we talk about it more, and be honest? We could remind each other that we are all trying together to lead a holy life. We can cheer each other on. We can confess that it is hard. We can talk about the incompleteness of our belief and our effort. That's when the grace can pour in. That's when we can be stitched back together. That is the very place of our strengthening.

Holiness never pretends. Pretending is a waste of time and a waste of love. If you're pretending to have it all together or to know things you don't know, please stop. "Life is too short to pretend," Brent would say. He was exactly right.

⌒

We must not wallow for long in all our failures at living into and out of holiness. These are the things that come to mind when we sit in a moment of quiet during a church service, before the confession, whatever that looks like in your church world. Or they are the things we think of when we visit our grandmothers and they look at us intently, with those eyes. In what could have been, we can see what might later be. This is a more hopeful way to understand the mistakes we make, all our misses and non-attempts at an intentional holy life. Our missteps are the material of our ongoing repentance.

One of the pastor's roles, whatever the tradition, is to remind us that God forgives us, over and over again. I keep the Book of Common Prayer—the one Brent used most Sundays—on the dresser we shared and into which we stuffed our sweaters and socks. The book is bound in red leather, beautiful and with a little weight to it. The pages have a top-edge gilt. After leading us all in the confession on one page, the leader flips to the very next page and reminds us that our God is merciful, that he pardons and delivers us from all our sins. They say the words that have been named comfortable. It is so lovely to use the word *comfortable* for lines like these: "Come to me, all who labor and are heavy laden, and I will give you rest."[2] They read out loud for all to hear that God confirms and strengthens us in all goodness, and will bring us to everlasting life. Whatever kind of church you hitch your holiness to, make sure it is one that reminds you of those things.

This is all so hopeful. Holiness says no to fear. Holiness says yes to hope.

Holiness grows from love's work, and the soft, reassuring touch of grace. Also, holiness asks us to believe that we can change. Do we have the courage to try? How would we treat our own bodies, and the bodies of other people, if we believed we were holy and so were they, softly shaped in God's image? How would we view our homes and our hospitality if we saw all the holy possibilities when we invite others in? Our money transforms in our very hands when we tangle with how we might be worshiping it. A hold examined can be a hold loosened. Holiness can impact everything, if we let it: the whole of our lives and all our loves. It takes a bit of work.

More consciously living a holy life can bring us the integration we long for between what we believe and how we live. Holiness is both our identity and our practice. Trying to live an intentionally holy life solves the disconnect so many of us can feel between our beliefs and our practice. On a Saturday morning, we cannot rush little old ladies with walkers down the buffet table, or finish their sentences because we are a bit of a know-it-all, watching the clock. When we work to control our rude and selfish selves, this takes discipline. The gift of love we give to someone else might be very hard work. We stretch. We shrink. We moan and we groan. That can sometimes be the way of holiness.

The people we serve or love with holiness might not have any idea that some effort was required by us, and that is just fine. We don't have to go around telling everyone what hard work they are. Or sighing when we look at them. We should notice what we are thinking, though, and how we are feeling. We can let the light into our own private rooms, and in that honest self-realization, draw nearer to God who has said clearly that nothing can separate us from the divine love. Forgiveness is always at hand for grouchy us.

Making holy space for others is the opposite of what a striving, self-focused culture can tell us to do. The path of holiness seems to almost always involve staying second in line longer than is comfortable.

The divine design of holiness will, ideally, lead us to discover our truest selves and live our best-despite-all-that-can-go-horribly-wrong lives, because we are living in response to God's love for us. We are living aware of our belovedness in such a way that it frees us to love others as well as we can. The relinquishment of first to second or even last in the buffet line will grow to feel more natural, as if this ordering, commanded, was also a way for us to receive God's love. Of course, some people might take advantage of that. There are always people who will gorge on our love. Losing ourselves is not decimating ourselves. Self-sacrifice is not self-sabotage. It is less of us and more of God; and then, beautifully and proportionately, we are simmered gently and slowly down into the beautiful essence of our truest selves. (If you make a certain kind of sauce, you know just what I mean.) Less is more. But if love poured out leaves us empty for too long or feels wrong in a way that lingers, careful attention is needed. It takes courage and freedom to say a heck no, as well as a holy yes.

We need to be our own dear friends and take care of ourselves, too. Being part of an intimate Christian community where people deeply know us and our daily lives can also help us know when it is time to wrap ourselves in a blanket and receive the holy care of others. Friends need to know what is happening so they can give to us and we can receive from them.

Some of us might also live in roles, for a time at least, that make sacrificial living less of a choice and more of what feels like a requirement. Young children don't even let us use the bathroom alone. There are some seasons in life that are full of joy and also feel like a training camp for sacrifice. There are times when we need to find our voices along with our love and speak up and ask for what we need to stay full and fulfilled. We need to watch out for one another and encourage each other to live out our highest and best callings, which can change with those seasons. Sisters, spouses, cousins, friends, bosses, and all the women and men who have done this work before and kneel beside us at church can help us discover this is true.

Raising children, I found my vocation as a writer. The boundaries of motherhood gave me space to be a writer. I wrote during naps, which made me quick. I wrote after bedtime, which made me tired, grouchy some mornings, but satisfied. I lived some of what I would later write about. I was being formed, and this would come in handy later. I acknowledge this blooming of two callings as rare and see how essential my husband was, his hand at my back, urging me forward into the fullness of my calling. We can do that for one another, and we should.

In losing ourselves, we should find ourselves, and we will all take good care of each other after all.

Every opportunity we find in front of us to live out of our holiness is also an opportunity to receive grace for all the ways we do not and cannot do it as we imagine ourselves doing it, like a super saint. We try to live holy, notice we aren't really doing that, reject shame, and instead sink back into grace, and then maybe grow one quarter of an inch, and thanks be to God for that. I think that's how this works. We do become more holy-ish over time. Our effort does lead us forward, along the path of grace and goodness. It is good to try to do hard and holy.

The authentic practice of holiness will help us nurture a brutal honesty about ourselves. Honesty is required. We know how we are feeling inside when we don't receive the attention or the thanks, the small round of applause for our little holy selves. I notice you not noticing me, and I notice that I am noticing. I can say to Jesus, "Help." Nothing grows in a straight line, and neither will our holiness.

⌒

It would be ideal if we were the only ones that our personal holiness made uncomfortable. And if this discomfort came because we were going one inch farther than we wanted to, which makes it the smallest of sacrifices. That might mean welcoming to our dinner table someone we barely know or, if given all the choices, before whom we would not have chosen to set our best plates. But we do it anyway because we see that hospitality can be holy, and so can listening and learning.

Holiness is about giving a glass of cold water to quench thirst, and then it's about asking ourselves and God why that was difficult, it if was. *What does that mean?* The answer can help us grow. We grow in holiness in this outward and then inward, inward and then outward fashion, and we do it best when we are together with others in the work of holiness.

Go to church. It can help. If it hurts you, find a different one with a pastor who is humble and kind and still honest and holy. There will always be people who are annoying. You are annoying. I am really annoying, and sometimes a lot of work. But we're still holy, and we still belong together.

One time in our church, I heard Genesis 3, when God tells Adam and Eve they must leave the Garden, read out loud in a stern voice. And I noticed that it surprised me.

There's no doubt this passage of Scripture is one of the bad bits of the Bible. Adam and Eve have eaten of the tree of knowledge. They've been caught red-handed. Running and hiding has now begun. Suffering has arrived. Banishment is at hand. There is now a chasm to be crossed. That Sunday, God sounded outraged and not like the heartbroken parent I had always imagined in that passage. Perhaps the reader was projecting. Perhaps so was I. My parents were gentle toward their daughters, which impacted my view of God. I might just be a flake, but I've always imagined God as sad in that story, and not mad. God did make clothes for them, after all.[3]

In that same way, when God says, "Be holy because I am holy,"[4] I hear it now as an invitation and not a stern Leviticus-style command. "Well, that's certainly a contemporary way of thinking about it," Brent said when I ran my theory past him. This told me we might not be on the same exact page with this thought. These are still good questions to ask: What if a non-yelling God is inviting us to be holy because it is good and beautiful for us and the world God loves? What if it's not about ruining all our fun? Can holiness heal us?

⌒

Paul reminds the Philippians and us to work our salvation out "with fear and trembling, for it is God who works in you to will and to act in order to fulfill his good purpose."[5] We are working out our salvation one way and then the other, with all our stumbles but also with small and sacred successes. We're not total wrecks. We do holy things. I see you being and doing holy, and you see me. We can cheer each other on in the gradual working out of love in our lives and in the world that needs this great and unmatchable love. We are each other's comfort and encouragement. We are sanctified by the hard things, but also by love. Sanctification does not always have to hurt. Love, too, helps make us holy.

Our beautiful, painful, joyful, and deeply surprising lives matter. We are part of the big plan and the big idea. All our loves and our sorrows, all that we gain and each thing we lose, are seen by Jesus, who is standing closely, paying attention. This I choose to believe. "Help my unbelief"[6] is a prayer to God and a request of each other. It's okay to have to try to believe over and over again. In that fragile place we kneel in good company.

We are part of God's unfolding story, unlikely us who are so seen and so loved. That story is stacked with saints of the ordinary who made one choice after another until, eventually, that leaning into and living out of holiness felt more like an impulse of their own belovedness and the very proof of how God can remake a life, and maybe less like a chore.

The opportunity to do small and sometimes very big and holy things is everywhere, all the time. Holiness is here, and it is now. Holiness is lived out in our lives between us and God, the true Holy One. Holiness is meant to be the warm love among one another. Holy is, and holy does. No matter who we have been and what we have done, or not yet done, it is surely never too late.

God warmly welcomes us. We are beckoned into the embrace of holiness. We are practicing holiness, and we are safe. And on the day when our holiness is complete and so, finally, is our joy, we will see our holy beloveds again, and maybe we really can cannonball into the river of life, and climb that magnificent tree.

DISCUSSION QUESTIONS

Chapter 1 | Searching for Holiness

1. If you're like me (and a lot of other people), it feels weird to think of yourself as holy. How comfortable, or uncomfortable, does this make you?

2. How have you been surprised by holiness showing up in an unexpected place or person?

3. What was a time when you did a hard and holy thing?

4. When you think about friends and family, who do you think of first when you think about someone who is holy? Why do you think that is?

Chapter 2 | Fruit

1. Is there a fruit of the Spirit—love, joy, peace, patience, kindness, goodness, faithfulness, gentleness, self-control—that you resonate with the most, either as one you can see in your own life or one you wish to see more of?

2. Have you ever made a personal decision to act in a certain way as consistently as possible over time? What role do you think that has played in the formation and development of the fruit of the Spirit in your life?

3. When you mess up, how easily can you see the opportunity for repentance and growth?

4. This chapter touches on heaven just a little bit (almost by accident, I confess). How does the idea of heaven as a kind of completion to our holiness impact your view of holiness here and now?

5. In this chapter, I write about naming my friend Hannah a writer because she needed it to be confirmed by someone else. Whom in your life could you confirm as holy and offer a gentle reminder?

Chapter 3 | Body

1. Have you ever had your feet washed in a church service? What was that like for you? What does it reveal about us and the way God loves us?

2. We all have a relationship with our own perception of our bodies and what they mean in our lives. Do you view your body as holy? How does that impact how you live, and how has that changed over the years?

3. How do you think your body, your holiness, and your relationship with God are connected?

4. "Holiness means being set apart, and this can be a drag." Explore that a bit, and see what comes up.

Chapter 4 | Money

1. Would you consider yourself a cheerful or a sometimes grouchy giver?

2. We live in a world that nurtures our envy and desire for more. What spiritual practices or holy thoughts do you use to counter that cultural obsession for more of everything?

3. Could you give away more? What would that feel and look like?

4. Whom could you engage in honest conversation about the challenges around money and possessions? What is the first thing you would want to discuss?

Chapter 5 | Hospitality

1. How do you practice hospitality in your life? How could you practice it more?

2. Hospitality can be uncomfortable if you worry too much, or if your guests are or become annoying as the evening wears on. How can our feelings about those kinds of things move us along into holiness?

3. How are your listening skills? What would someone who loves you but wants you to grow tell you about your listening skills?

4. "Moving against the impulse toward our own comfort can be part of how we grow and become our best selves. What if we are shortchanging ourselves when we don't stretch

ourselves?" How true do you think these statements are? What is the balance in your life between stretching and simply doing too much?

Chapter 6 | Humility

1. In this chapter I tell the story about eating my potato and my classmate taking pity on me and asking me to walk her through a chapel. Have there been times when you thought you were being fabulous, and then learned maybe it wasn't all about you after all?

2. "Our great and tiny and repeated humbling is part of the nonlinear growth path of holiness." How has this been true (or not true) for you?

3. The stamp story is so small. I gave away a stamp and then regretted it. That showed me I was nice, but not as nice as I like to imagine. Do you have a story like that you feel safe to share, or even just reflect upon?

4. Is the idea of doing the holy opposite of what you might be first inclined to do a new thought to you? Does it feel like a possible practice to take on?

Chapter 7 | Beauty

1. Can you name and describe a place so beautiful that you felt transcendent and moved by the experience of simply being in it?

2. In what ways does beauty give you hope?

3. How does the idea of very ordinary things and moments—like a walk down the road on a sunny day—impact your idea of what is holy in the world and in yourself?

4. What do you think about the role of mutual encouragement in a holy life? Whom could you encourage in their holiness? Who could encourage you?

5. What beautiful thing can you make for Jesus?

Chapter 8 | Church

1. Was there a time when you really disliked church? Why do you think that was (or is)?

2. Do you feel you have things in common with the people at your church? What does that mean to you? In what ways does it matter?

3. My church is Anglican (in case you hadn't guessed), and therefore it has a structure and a liturgy that helps draw me into worship and reminds me of God's holiness, and our dependence on God for our own holiness. How does your tradition's structure or flavor impact your experience of holiness?

4. Church, and church people, can be so disappointing. How have you been disappointed by church? How have you been restored?

Chapter 9 | Remembering

1. What is your warmest and dearest memory from your faith journey? If you built an ebenezer, where and when would it be?

2. What is your favorite memory from the Bible? A story that moved you, sustained you, and taught you something crucial for your own faith journey?

3. "Our memories of encounters with God's holiness can sustain us for our own journey deeper in and further out, into our own holy callings in the world." How has this been true for you? How could it be?

4. When have you had to be very strong in your life? How did holy memories help you?

Chapter 10 | Sorrow

1. This was a difficult but essential chapter for me to write. My husband died after I had written nine chapters for this book, and I couldn't not write about such a cataclysmic event. Brent has always been part of my work and an essential part of my faith life. I couldn't leave him or his death out of this book. Other writers might have made a different choice. Did our story stir up your own grief? What or who have been your great losses?

2. There are a lot of clichés around grief and suffering, and platitudes that aren't helpful. What did help me, and my family, were the people who showed up and just did stuff and loved us. What has your experience been like, either of showing up in other people's times of suffering or of being attended to in yours? How have you experienced God—or felt God was absent for a time—during pain and suffering?

3. Whom should you run off to see and visit, and to remind them that you love them? Consider doing that right now.

Chapter 11 | Holiness Here and Now

1. Holy living happens on purpose. How can you lead your holy life on purpose?

2. "Our missteps are the material of our ongoing repentance." In what ways have you learned from your missteps and mistakes in this life of holiness?

3. "Living a holy life does not need to be complicated. It can be simple." How do you feel about that?

4. What do you think you need in order to lead your specific holy life?

ACKNOWLEDGMENTS

PEOPLE WHO KNOW ME WELL were surprised I was writing a book about holiness. I don't seem very holy—in a stereotypical way—most of the time. But that's part of the puzzle I was trying to solve. As with all my writing projects, I began by reading other books to try to understand. My husband, Brent, brought home books about holiness from his office library for me, and then would check in every now and then to make sure I was caring for them properly and ask if I was done with his books yet. We were like that with each other: the most honest of companions, and deeply in love through the ups and downs and from the beginning to the end that came far too soon.

I want to acknowledge Brent first and always for the gift of the life we lived together and how it formed us. He showed me that we can be holy and flawed, made whole and still broken at the same time, because it's all about grace. He loved me so well. Thank you, sweetheart.

This book began with a question that followed a prayer. My friend Michelle Terwilliger, who worked alongside my husband, prayed: "Give us grace, God, to lead a holy life." And from my seat in the pew, I felt curious about what that might mean. I suspect that's how many books begin. Thank you, Pastor Michelle, for that and for everything.

The parish of St. Peter and St. Paul's Anglican Church in Ottawa will forever be in my heart. You are everywhere through this book. I hope you see that, and I hope it's okay. I am one of many writers and artists who have called that church home. I will never forget you or your love.

I needed help at various points in this book to believe that I might have something to contribute to the long conversation about holiness, and to simply keep going. Thank you to Charlotte Donlon, spiritual director for writers, who met with me over several sessions and helped me find my courage. Ilana Reimer (a young writer to watch), and Susan Fish and Patricia Paddey (seasoned writers to read), each stepped in to comment on a rough, unfinished manuscript. Thank you also to my friend Renata Ellis, who read an early version of the book and cheered me on. You each helped me not give up, and you made my work better. Thank you.

Writers Jen Pollock Michel and Nicole Parsons asked good questions of scenes I shared with them in our small writing group. Thank you for the push I needed to try to do better. It's always about the revision. The writing group of St. Peter and St. Paul's was always encouraging. How good it is for writers to meet together.

My agent, Hilary McMahon, is so helpful and encouraging, also firm and no-nonsense, which is exactly what you want in an agent. She's also kind. She sat with me in my sorrow and brought mc soup. Thank you, Hilary, for helping me continue to become a writer.

The team at NavPress were patient, kind, and flexible. They sent flowers when Brent died, and that was the only bouquet I carried upstairs to our bedroom. When I woke up in the morning and saw it on our dresser, it gave me some hope that I had good work for my hands and heart and that there would be a dot of light far off in the distance. In the early months of grief, I had meaningful work to do, and I believe that helped me. Shortly after I submitted the manuscript, I attended an author retreat hosted by their small and mighty team. I met other authors and saw I was in very good company. I also met with my editor, Deborah Gonzalez, assuming we'd begin to dissect the book over coffee. Instead, we shared some of our stories with each other, and I left knowing I was working with someone I could trust. That proved to be true. Thank you, Deborah, for making this book better and for asking me such good questions. Thank you also to David Zimmerman, Olivia Eldredge, and the rest of the NavPress team, along with the skilled crew at Tyndale House, who, through the unique partnership between houses, played an essential role.

Jeff Crosby, whom I've only met once in person, has been a constant source of encouragement and practical help. He has been a friend to me as he is to so many other writers and exemplifies what it means to be a writer's writer. I am grateful.

An unexpected thing happened to me after the publication of my first book, *The Minister's Wife*. I began to hear from readers who emailed me to tell me they felt less alone. On behalf of writers everywhere, let me say that such feedback is gold, because then you also feel less alone. To know your work is being read and has resonated in some small way is a beautiful thing (which can actually feel a little bit holy). Such feedback helped me continue along my writing journey. Thank you.

Too many friends and family to name encouraged and cared for me and our family in our time of need, which was also eventually, for me, a time of writing. You brought us cups of water. We are grateful beyond measure.

Our children—Thomas, Holly, Erik, and his wife, Nicoli—told me I could finish a book that I started in one life and ended in another. Thank you for standing by your mom. Thank you for reminding me of what remains holy and good in life. Your dad would be so proud of you. I am so proud of you.

NOTES

CHAPTER 1 | SEARCHING FOR HOLINESS

1. J. I. Packer, *Rediscovering Holiness: Know the Fullness of Life with God* (Grand Rapids, MI: Baker Books, 2014), 157.
2. My friend is Darryl Dash. You can find his work at www.dashhouse.com.
3. "J. C. Ryle," 5 Minutes in Church History with Stephen Nichols, accessed January 26, 2022, https://www.5minutesinchurchhistory.com/j-c-ryle.
4. J. C. Ryle, *Holiness: Its Nature, Hindrances, Difficulties, and Roots* (Peabody, MA: Hendrickson Publishers, 2007), 110.
5. From the Book of Common Prayer (2019), available here: https://bcp2019.anglicanchurch.net.
6. 1 Peter 3:9, NIV.
7. J. I. Packer, *Rediscovering Holiness*, 151.
8. John 20:4.
9. John 20:17.
10. John 20:18.

CHAPTER 2 | FRUIT

1. John R. W. Stott, *Baptism and Fullness: The Work of the Holy Spirit Today*, 3rd ed. (Downers Grove, IL: InterVarsity Press, 1964, 2006), 76.
2. 1 Corinthians 13:12.
3. 1 Peter 2:9.
4. Zechariah 14:20-21.
5. 1 Peter 2:5.

CHAPTER 3 | BODY

1. From the Book of Common Prayer (2019), available here: https://bcp2019.anglicanchurch.net.

2. Acts 17:28.
3. Romans 12:1-2.
4. Psalm 139:14.

CHAPTER 4 | MONEY
1. Matthew 6:24, NRSV.
2. 2 Corinthians 9:7.
3. As described here: https://snscasinotours.com/portfolio-item/royal-caribbean
-allure.
4. Matthew 6:33-34.
5. Matthew 6:19-21, NKJV.
6. Hebrews 10:24.
7. Acts 20:35.

CHAPTER 5 | HOSPITALITY
1. From the Book of Common Prayer (2019), available here: https://bcp2019
.anglicanchurch.net.
2. John 1:1.

CHAPTER 6 | HUMILITY
1. Matthew 5:13-16, NIV.
2. Romans 12:10, NIV.
3. Philippians 2:6-8, NIV.
4. 1 Peter 5:6.

CHAPTER 7 | BEAUTY
1. Matthew 6:26, NIV.
2. Isaiah 40:31; Matthew 10:16.
3. Jeremiah 18:6.
4. Psalm 146.
5. Luke 7:38, NIV.
6. Matthew 26:6-13.

CHAPTER 8 | CHURCH
1. Matthew 22:37-40, NIV.
2. 1 Corinthians 12:15.
3. 1 Timothy 3:2.
4. From the Book of Common Prayer (2019), available here: https://bcp2019
.anglicanchurch.net.
5. Hebrews 10:23-25, ESV.

CHAPTER 9 | REMEMBERING

1. Philippians 1:6, NIV.
2. 1 John 1:1, NIV.
3. Psalm 103:12.
4. Psalm 103:2-5.
5. From the Book of Common Prayer (2019), available here: https://bcp2019 .anglicanchurch.net.
6. Psalm 143:6.

CHAPTER 10 | SORROW

1. John 11:25-26, as quoted in the Book of Common Prayer (2019), available here: https://bcp2019.anglicanchurch.net.

CHAPTER 11 | HOLINESS HERE AND NOW

1. 2 Timothy 1:9, NIV.
2. Matthew 11:28, ESV. As quoted in the Book of Common Prayer (2019), available here: https://bcp2019.anglicanchurch.net.
3. "The LORD God made garments of skin for Adam and his wife and clothed them," Genesis 3:21, NIV.
4. 1 Peter 1:16.
5. Philippians 2:12-13, NIV.
6. Mark 9:24, ESV.

NavPress is the book-publishing arm of The Navigators.

Since 1933, The Navigators has helped people around the world bring hope and purpose to others in college campuses, local churches, workplaces, neighborhoods, and hard-to-reach places all over the world, face-to-face and person-by-person in an approach we call Life-to-Life® discipleship. We have committed together to know Christ, make Him known, and help others do the same.®

Would you like to join this adventure of discipleship and disciplemaking?

- Take a Digital Discipleship Journey at **navigators.org/disciplemaking**.
- Get more discipleship and disciplemaking content at **thedisciplemaker.org**.
- Find your next book, Bible, or discipleship resource at **navpress.com**.

 @NavPressPublishing

 @NavPress

 @navpressbooks

CP1790